Arias

Arias

Sharon Olds

Alfred A. Knopf   New York   2019

THIS IS A BORZOI BOOK
PUBLISHED BY ALFRED A. KNOPF

www.aaknopf.com

Knopf, Borzoi Books, and the colophon are registered
trademarks of Penguin Random House LLC.

Library of Congress Cataloging-in-Publication Data
Names: Olds, Sharon, author.
Title: Arias / by Sharon Olds.
Description: First edition. | New York : Knopf, 2019. | "This is a
Borzoi book."
Identifiers: LCCN 2019007458 (print) | LCCN 2019008791 (ebook) |
ISBN 9780525656944 (ebook) | ISBN 9780525656937 (hardcover) |
ISBN 9781524711603 (paperback)
Subjects: | BISAC: POETRY / American / General.
Classification: LCC PS3565.L34 (ebook) | LCC PS3565.L34 A6 2019
(print) | DDC 811/.54—dc23
LC record available at https://lccn.loc.gov/2019007458

Jacket photograph by TK
Jacket design by TK

Manufactured in the United States of America
First Edition

For Carolyn and Forrest

Contents

Run Away Up

Elegies

1

2

3

First Child

Meeting a Stranger

For You

In the morning, when I'm pouring the hot milk
into the coffee, I put the side of my
face near the convex pitcher, to watch
the last, round drop from the spout—
and it feels like being cheek to cheek
with a baby. Sometimes the orb pops back up,
a ball of cream balanced on a whale's
watery exhale. Then I gather the tools
of my craft, the cherry sounding-board tray
for my lap, like the writing-arm of a desk,
the phone, the bird book for looking up
the purple martin. I repeat them as I seek them,
so as not to forget: tray, cell phone,
purple martin; tray, phone,
martin, Trayvon Martin, song was
invented for you, all art was made
for you, painting, writing, was yours,
our youngest, our most precious, to remind us
to shield you—all was yours, all that is
left on earth, with your body, was for you.

Looking South at Lower Manhattan,
Where the Towers Had Been

If we see harm approaching someone—
if you see me starting to talk about
something I know nothing about,
like the death of someone who's a stranger to me,
step between me and language. This morning,
I am seeing it more clearly, that song
can be harmful, in its ignorance
which does not know itself as ignorance.
I have crossed the line, as the line was crossed
with me. I need to apologize
to the letters of the alphabet,
to the elements of the periodic
table, to O, and C, and H,
oxygen, carbon, hydrogen,
which make up most of a human body—
body which breaks down, in fire,
to the elements it was composed of, and all that is
left is ashes, sacred ashes
of strangers, carbon and nitrogen,
and the rest departs as carbon dioxide and is
breathed in, by those nearby,
the living who knew us and the living who did not
know us. I apologize
to nitrogen, to calcium with the
pretty box-shape of its crystal structure,
I apologize to phosphorus,
and potassium, that raw bright metal
we contain, and to sodium and sulfur, and to
the trace amounts which are in us somewhere like the
stars in the night—copper, zinc,
cobalt, iron, arsenic, lead,
I am singing, I am singing against myself, as if
rushing toward someone my song might be approaching,
to shield them from it.

Meeting a Stranger

When I meet you, it's not just the two of us meeting.
Your mother is there, and your father is there,
and my mother and father. And our people—back from our
folks, back—are there, and what they
might have had to do with each other;
if one of yours, and one of mine
had met, what might have happened is there
in the room with us. They are shadowy,
compared to us, they are quivers of reflected
light on a wall. And if I were
a German, and you a Jew, or I a
Jew and you a Palestinian,
or, as this morning, when you are an African
American woman, and I am a WASP,
one of your family might have been taken
from their home, and brought through murder to murder
by one of my family. It is there in the air
with us. And if you're a woman in the city
where you live, and I am staying at
the hotel where you work, and if you have brought me
my breakfast on a tray—though you and I have not
met, before, we are breathing in
our lineages, together. And whether
there is guilt in the room, or not, or blame,
there is the history of human evil,
and the shame, in me, that someone I could be
related to, could have committed,
against someone you are related to, some
horror. And in the room, there is
a question, alive—would I have risked harm
to try to protect you, as I hope I would risk it
for a cousin, a niece, or would I have stood
aside, in the ordinary cowardice and self-
interest of my flesh now sharing your breath,
your flesh my breath.

No Makeup

Maybe one reason I do not wear makeup is to scare people.
If they're close enough, they can see something is different with me,
something unnerving, as if I have no features,
I am embryonic, pre-eyebrows, pre-eyelids, pre-mouth,
I am like a water bear talking to them,
or an amniotic traveler,
a vitreous floater on their own eyeball,
human ectoplasm risen on its hind legs to discourse with them.
And such a white white girl, such a sickly toadstool,
so pale, a visage of fog, a phiz of
mist above a graveyard, no magenta roses,
no floral tribute, no goddess, no grown-up
woman, no acknowledgment
of the drama of secondary sexual characteristics, just the
gray matter of spirit talking,
the thin features of a gray girl in a gray graveyard—
granite, ash, chalk, dust.
I tried the paint, but I could feel it on my skin, I could
hardly move, under the mask of my
desire to be seen as attractive in the female
way of 1957,
and I could not speak. And when the makeup came off I felt
actual as a small mammal in the woods
with a speaking countenance—or a basic
primate, having all the expressions
which evolved in us, to communicate.
If my teenage acne had left scars,
if my skin were rough, instead of soft,
I probably couldn't afford to hate makeup,
or to fear so much the beauty salon or the
very idea of beautyship.
And my mother was beautiful—did I say this?
In my small eyes, and my smooth withered skin,
you can see my heart, you can read my naked lips.

A Pair of Sonnets Against the Corporal Chastisement of Children

Blows That Fall on a Child

Blows don't fall. Feathers fall,
and are dropped from towers. Leaves fall.
Dictionaries fall from towers—
the speed of their fall accelerates,
and the rate of the acceleration
accelerates. What falls is something
let go of, something gravity
is hauling to it, to *tiramisu* it—
dessert that says *pull me to you.* The liver
and lights of the body that the blow strikes are not
magnets, the blow is neither drawn
to its objects nor floated down from its source—
a blow is driven, by an engine, it is
the expression of a heart.

The Progeny of Punishment

They inherit the earth. They crawl on it,
they pull themselves up, they walk, they look up,
they do not know which visage they will see
above them—the crescent, or the waxing gibbous,
seas and craters of the eyes nose mouth.
Sometimes the cycle has a pattern, sometimes
the new is followed in an instant by the full,
as if a face turned suddenly toward you,
and in its holes and shadows you could read
the next hour of your life. With the impact of a
giant bolide, the moon was born,
struck right off the earth. The children
born as the corporeal subjects of their makers
are our species' living daylights, being beaten out.

(b. 1972, d. 1979)

1.

Poem to Etan Patz

> Then the butter we put on our white bread
> was colored with butter yellow, a cancerous dye,
> and all the fourth graders were taken by streetcar
> to the Dunky Company to see milk processed.
> ... Before we were herded back to the streetcar line,
> we were each given a half pint of milk in tiny
> milk bottles with straws to suck it up. In this way
> we gradually learned about our country.
>
> —Ruth Stone, "American Milk"

This morning, on the front page, in a headline,
the *A* and the *Z* of your name. I was walking up the
sidewalk my son had walked up, that morning,
to the bus to school. I beg your forgiveness
for speaking to you now whom I had not known—
only my son, your age then, known.
And this morning there is an arrest, a confession,
now we have some words of a story,
lured, promise, bag, out in the
open with trash. He says you were
a block away from your building—not you,
but what you had been ravaged from.
But how could he have seen you, and wanted
to stop you, to tear you out of the world.
33 years ago—a
long life set next to yours.
Your mother, your father—forgive me, I do not
know them—may have walked past your folded
form. Young darling, nothing in your nature
had anything to do with anything you saw
that day, or learned. But who could want that,
for a baby to have to know, with his life, who we
are at our worst, with his last eyes—

your smile printed, then, on every
carton of what makes the bones long,
every child at breakfast gazing
into the red mirror. In this way
we gradually learn about our country.

2.

Poem Which Talks Back to Me

The parents whose boy went off to school
that morning—the police may have found someone
who saw their son, alive, after
they saw him for the last time. *Step away!*
Someone who saw that elfin face
change, at the word "soda." *Step back!*
And change again, and change. And down
the basement steps, down into the earth,
the stairs down into the underworld.
Don't go there. Close your eyes. Someone
may know the unbearable—someone
in custody. O, "custody."
A wall of dirt, a wall of stone,
a bare bulb, like the uterus upside
down. No Kaddish, no washing of the dead,
no linen shroud, no company
through the long night.
Whatever honor can be kept for him—
his pure and whole honor is kept
by his parents, for the rest of the hard
labor of their lives. All this time,
they could not die, so they'd be here, in case
he came back. *Unspeakable.* And now,
the one taken in for questioning cries out,
"I don't know why, I don't know why."
He will not tell. He is holding that hour

to himself. Did he hold that child in his hands. And
vanish him, the spirit mattered away.
And the dear matter—*don't*. The truck,
the landfill, or the barge, the burial
at sea—the dispersal, the containment within
the bounds of the oceans, crested on top and
cragged at the floor where the mantle of the planet pours
up, molten, through fissures—contained
in the air bound by the atmosphere, the
clouds of mourning pressing against
the inner surface of the casing. *Shut
your mouth. Put down your pen. Drop
your weapon! Stop! In the name of the law
and the prophets.* At his birth, the history of the earth began.

Birds in Alcoves

More and more, along the shore
of the Northeast Corridor,
where the trains run along the edge of the land,
birds are standing in alcoves like telephone booths
as the humans go by—
doorless ceilingless closets in walls of reed
whose floors are the banks, awash in water,
of inlets and bays.
Large wading birds step back into green recesses,
and stand very still,
sometimes more than one in the narrow space,
sometimes a blue heron and a great egret facing each other
beak to beak. Some birds do not stand,
but grip a branch with their feet to stay upright.
Some birds hop, bouncing along
like little pocketless kangaroos,
and a crow walks along with coins singing in her trousers.
But many birds
freeze when they see us,
like a horror movie—a scene in a house
where a killer has a special room.
Herons, egrets, ibises, bitterns,
storks, cranes, coots, rails
fall silent, struck motionless at our advent.
Some sidestep, for safekeeping, into extinction.

8 Moons

An atom bomb—does it reduce everything
to atoms—to a mist the size of the moon?
And the hydrogen bomb—is there water in it?
When you drop it, does the mushroom above it
look like a splash, as if you'd dropped
the moon onto the ocean? If you dropped
the moon onto the Pacific, would its
diameter fit? Eight moons
dropped onto the Pacific would fit on it.
We can't imagine the length of time
it took to make the universe.
And the death of the earth—for most of us,
unimaginable, and therefore
inevitable. As if each parent,
at the same moment, will see our offspring
atomized, our species' clouds
lifting off the globe, the huge, childless atom.

My Father's Whiteness

It takes me a lifetime to see my father
as a white man—to see his whiteness
(named by white men after gleaming and brightness).
I saw the muck sweat of his pallor, he'd be
faceup on the couch like a mushroom in a mushroom-forcer,
and I didn't even wonder what it would feel like
for a person to be proud of their father.
I knew that at the interfraternity council
he'd been the handsome, wisecracking one, the
president, proud he could not read,
he could always get someone to do that for him—
he liked to say the two people allowed
to graduate from his college without knowing how to
read or write were him and Herbert Hoover.
Nor did any frat house there
house a brother.
Nor did I see my father—that in order to pass
out every night on the couch, snore
and snort and gargle-sing from his chintz
sty, he had to overcome
every privilege known to a man
tall, dark, handsome, white,
straight, middle class. He had to put his
every advantage down on the street and drive
over it with that thump a tire
and a body make. O say can you see him as I
see him now, as if he had no one
to answer to, he so prepared
to devour and excrete the hopes he'd been handed
on a platter, the spoon in his mouth, he could eat
what he had not earned, he could do it in his sleep.

State Evidence

When the men in maximum security
were saying what they'd done, I thought of him,
the one who had not had a name
until they found our seventh-grade classmate's
body half buried near his brother's cabin
in the hills, fifty years ago, and for a
moment I thought that he had cheated, by paying
up front, not doing his time—the forty
thousand volts had sprung him from his twenty-four
hours a day, his four hundred thirty-eight
thousand hours. I do not know
how much it cost the state to fry him,
to light up a man like a city, a species, but it
probably wasn't as much as three
hots for fifty years, so his murder may have
saved us a lot, and it saved him a hell of a
lot of time. But his execution—
wasn't it state evidence that it's
O.K. to kill someone? What did she
have to protect herself with, against such
evidence? One pink
plastic barrette—hold the lamb,
or rabbit, in your fist, and sink
its shank in his throat. For a moment, I can feel it,
the desire that his memory of what happened
be snuffed, I can see how it could have felt
intolerable that he get to make a
whole new skin, every seven years—
to weave it in solitude, and eat it,
weave it and eat it,
except, as he lived, inside, there might have been a
daughter, outside, still living, because
we had not set our citizens, with him,
the example of slaughter.

Sweet Land of Liberty

The refuse bag, caught in a tree
down there, high in a bare locust,
like the skin of a figure, the flay—is wild
in the gusts this morning, impaled on the branches
like butcher-bird prey on thorns, it has the fringes of a
pelt, a coat in a strong wind.
A ghost *is* a coat, with a no one
wearing it. Sometimes the ghost of the
human is dressed in a white sheet,
at night, bringing his bowels to where they will be
gratified. Twisting, shuddering,
rippling as if whipped into frenzy,
writhing in the lay-wasting
of a thrashing, of being threshed like a field,
harrowed—the split sack, for an hour,
is crazed in motion like a being chained over
a fire. People have been raised on stakes
at the gates of cities, for ravens and crows
to eat, alive, people have been draped on
fences of barbed wire, to show
the qualities of the mind of the one who in-
side the fence presidents.
The garment of a member of our family is fluttering,
this morning, from a tree. What family?
Family of whom? My country, 'tis of thee.

White Woman in White Makeup

When the stylist backstage had given me white
makeup—not the greenish-pink
gray of my skin, but a bone-chalk ivory—
and black eyebrows, I looked in the mirror
and I thought, I see a dead white person.
But I don't want to wear blusher, or sunburn—
having been the homely child
of a white pretty mother,
I want to be featureless, a spirit
whose face somehow reflects the face
facing her. I want to look
harmless! The smart, shy, pale
girl in our class—the milk-toast white man
abducted her, and r. and m.
her, and in the hills, buried her.
Her mother, and father, and younger sister
lived in the bright light of our eyes,
flashbulbs, horror, for months, years, and the
killer was fried to death in a chair
like someone shut in the hinged, bronze
hollow bull Heliogabalus
wheeled over the coals of a fire.
If I had to see my face while I am
writing this, I would not write it.
When I was a child, I was encouraged to speak
from behind a tree as if I were the tree,
or speak as if up from out of the ground,
or, as a white adult, to speak
out from within a white adult—how
easy that has made my life is almost invisible to me.

Apocalypse Approaching as I'm Aging

First of all, sound went,
well before sight. All around me
the visible—the black-and-white
markings of the hairy and downy,
like hieroglyphs, like characters
in Hebrew, or in Arabic, coming
in from the right side of the page
as if from the future.
When I walked, I could not hear my footsteps,
something was shushing everything,
it was the end of the world, reaching back
like the silence when you leave a lover
who's impossible, but whom you love,
or the quiet the day before your best friend dies—
crows, crows, in the sky, or the eerie
absence of sound when you realize
you're smart, all along you've been smart, your ignorance
has been the knowledge that you don't know
what you don't know, like a form of intelligence,
and now near the end of the world you under-
stand things, you yourself
eschatological, you sense
the doctrine of final things. It is like
a religious conversion—from non-belief
in your own beauty and strength, to sudden
belief—the light on the road no longer
covering the center of every dream, but
you yourself are a light—it's like
falling in love with yourself, the one
who had been the villain. When I understand
that the world will end, that we will have made it
unlivable for ourselves, the birds
look so smooth, the sloped shoulders of the
woodpecker motionless on the mound of suet
who sleeps, like a baby on the breast—head
up, eyes shut, she sleeps,
at peace, near the end of the world.

My Godlessness

Before I was born, my godlessness
was not the pouch in which my mother
carried me inside her. My godlessness
was not the sperm, me sitting on one
dolphin shoulder slope of it,
my femaleness sitting on the other,
nor was my godlessness the palace
of the egg, cream-rich Twinkie. Nor was it
her milk, nor did I drink it with her milk—
nor the local church, carved of redwood,
like a tree with a door carved through at the base,
nor the beaten-gold cross on the altar,
the hammer-blows visible in it
like the hammered copper of my father's humidor.
My mother beating me was not the source
of my godlessness. The source was not
the rape and murder of my classmate, or the rapes
and murders of our fellow citizens.
It was not earth, or water, or air.
It was eternal fire. It was my permanent home
when I died, the licking of the tongues of fire.
The source of my godlessness was cruelty
and abuse of power, its minions were like the
flame-headed one roaring now
from the pulpit, the orange-haired extinctor.

Seas to Rise Forty Feet

There is so much water in a person. There is so much
air in an egg. As it heats, in the saucepan,
bubbles trickle out every pore.
The rectangle of suet in the feeder
is a dome, now, like the last, little,
rough, golden hill of earth
once the waters will cover us,
and the paper wasp I let the spider
stun, and swaddle in silk, and keep
alive all night, and eat, is now
a black and yellow cruciform
reaching out one double-length
golden arm
motionless
in protest of death. But death gave us
sex! and birth! I never understood that at the
end of the world, the songs would die
too, all the poems will die,
all the art. The maker of
the ashen pyriform of paper
dangles, still, this morning, early
proof of death without birth.

Arias

Aria to Our Miscarried One, Age 50 Now

Once again, I turn and address you,
not knowing who you were or what
you were. You had been three months inside me,
when a guest came to visit, with her virus,
which I caught—or your inviableness
may have been conceived with you,
you might have been, from the beginning, going to
last just fourteen weeks, though I had felt,
as we lay on the living room floor, the couch
pushed in front of the door at the pure gold
hour at the core of your big sister's
nap, that you had taken deep.
I kept my feet up on the couch an hour—there was a
recipe, for a boy, then:
abstain until the egg emerges, then
send the long-tailed whippersnapper, the
boy-making sperm, in, to get there
before the girls, who are slow, but if they
get there early can wait. The boy
we conceived, a month after you departed,
made, years later,
an ink X
on a cushion of that sofa, as if to declare
war on sisters and mothers, the oppressors
of the male. Hello, male, or female,
or both, or neither. Hi mystery,
hi matter, hi spirit moving through matter.
Twenty years ago, when your father
left me, I wanted to hold hands with you,
my friend in death, the dead one I'd known
best—and not at all—who had
deserted this life or been driven from it,
I your garden, oasis, desert.
And I'd never laid down a stone for you,
you seemed like a byway on the path from your sister
to your brother. You who were part-formed,

how close I could have felt to you if I'd
known what a hidden story I still
was to myself. Dear one, I feel
as if you're my elder, you having departed—
though without having breathed—much earlier than I.
By the time I saw you, you were back in the ocean
already, the sacred toilet-water green
of your grave. Let me call you kin, lost one,
let me call you *landsman*.

Aria Above Seattle

About to land—in the state which used to be
islands, till the ocean floor dove under
the continent, bringing the masses
of rock in, to dock—I remember
that my father is buried here. Not his hair,
twenty years long in the grave, not his body
distilled by the soil's rotgut,
but his ashes—for the first time in years I am near
my father's bones, ground and rendered,
and I want to go in, where they are, and play among their
ochre spheres, as if I could be in a
stone tumbler with him, or soar,
fellow solar orbiter,
inside an atom of his, neutrons
and protons and electrons of his ungainsayable
existence—there can never be a world, here,
whatever happens, in which my father will have
not existed. I want to say
I loved my father, always, on the
molecular level—I love the word
love, I want to wear it as
the human clothing, though I know I do not
know what it means for someone to love, to
honor, their father and mother. Well,
I will hold to the geological record,
here is where the mantle bent,
here is where the magma came up
through the mile of glacier. And I feel that if I could
hold some of those tiny, round
dice of his calcium and marrow I might be
feeling what any girl on a playground
would feel with her beloved marbles. I know—
wanting the animal evidence
in my palm, as if to own, to dote,
spiritless, on matter . . . but I have
my hopes of what could come, for me, from
knowing there are forms of love
unknowable to me.

Anal Aria

When John Gardner said, to a crowd
of writers, "All writers are anal,"
I had never heard the word *anal.*
And I'd just heard there were women who preferred
to be "fucked in the ass," and men who preferred,
in women, the ass. And I'd seen the beauty
of my father's face, in makeup, when he'd cross-
dressed, the breasts especially fully expressed,
every Hallowed Eve. And I thought
Gardner might mean that the best writers
want to fuck, or be fucked, in the ass, and I worried about that.
The ass . . . When my kids had been two, or three, they would
watch their poop circle, and spiral
down, and they would wave goodbye.
And now that my apartment has a narrow-exit toilet,
I may stand and watch the drama, the level
of the pool sinking, the toilet paper
pulling apart into transparent wings in that pre-
Stygian greenish element, then
drawn into the tunnel down 17 stories to the
pipes under the streets where men stand up
with alligators, and keep political
prisoners, to rend information
out of them. If my mom had not beat me while I
clenched my butt as if to keep her out,
I might have liked the asshole more, I might
want to kiss it! I have been away
from sex so long I don't remember much—
surely two people could kiss each other's
ass at the same time. The great
bouquet of the body, its floral parts,
alveolar plate to anuz, *A*
to *Z*, conception to death, begin to make
a ring a rosy, pocket full a
posy, around me, until I all fall
down—nectar, nectar; ashes, ashes.

Bay Area Aria

Someone said, Do you miss the Bay Area,
and suddenly I adored the phrase *the Bay Area*,
as if *area* were a newly made word
made between a body of water and a shore,
still fresh from its making, still washed by the Bay.
Do I miss the Bay Area? If it had felt as if I belonged to it,
I would miss it to death—
not the sight of the prison where people
waited to be roasted in metal chairs by the State and its God—
but the diesel water licking Emeryville,
the sea lions on Seal Rock below Cliff House,
the thousands of kinds of trees like a cloth factory with
millions of bolts of leaf-shapes and cone-patterns;
and the insects, the bees, dragons, damsels, wasps, hornets, flies;
eucalyptus tearing off her clothes in pieces,
her little blue socket-knocker hatboxes,
the live-oaks billion pen-point nib-needles,
the trees' shadows like dropped black skirts under them
on the burnt-grass ground.
Someone said to me in the Bay Area,
You must miss Galway a lot, and I frowned, I didn't like that,
and I said, If I thought
he was never coming back,
I'd be so bereft, so angry at God, as if the
world had been taken from me when Galway had left.
I know what he gave us will stay with us—
but he is never coming back. I know that this
had never been our permanent home.
It's a wild dance, hands grasping and
letting go and grasping. And I am never coming back.
I am not leaving, and I'm not coming back.

Bonnard Aria

It wasn't a date, I don't know how we ended
up, there, at MoMA, together,
I don't know which painting we were standing in front of—
gilded, plump, wiggle-lipped cream-pitcher,
ladies' hair like naked-lady
nether-hair, and the most erotic
light I had seen, I was nineteen, I turned
and kissed his mouth and held him. His eyebrows
went up, he was gorgeous, a grad student, almost
silent, I didn't know about such things,
he was seriously depressed, young darling—to me then like
an older man, twenty-four,
big and graceful. His face opened and we
took the old hot filthy summer
subway to his small, dark
apartment with its single bed.
I told him I couldn't really sleep with him,
he did not seem to mind. This was the
first time I had watched and felt
a naked penis grow. And it happened
that he had a big penis, not so
big as to be scary, but it had a solemn
majesty, a sublimity,
I felt I could have fainted, it was the sweetest
most moving thing I had seen. Standing
for no one but himself, standing not even
for himself, representing no one, nothing,
he welcomed me to our nakedness
where the painful apartness of our genderedness
was tenderly relieved, with intimate grandeur.
How many months how many years later
did he make his way
off the earth,
out of his life, pulling his life out
after him, destroying the breath and
motion of the evidence.

I had never thanked him—I have never thanked him.
How can I thank him. The closest I can come
is by giving something—anything—
to someone else—to anyone.

Breaking Bad Aria

When I become addicted to *Breaking Bad*—
he gets sexually aroused by cooking meth and having
killed someone, it excites him so much he fucks
harder than he has ever fucked—
I wonder how many men find such things
exciting, and why do I like the show
so much? I get to look at murder,
and its leftovers, the sock-knitting eggs
of the renal glands, outside the body,
what had been cherished wasted, debauched,
the bathtub, with the man's half-dissolved corpse,
falling through the floor eaten by the solvent,
through the ceiling downstairs, the body contempted,
I get to see the innards unprivate, I
get to watch it pretend. But it isn't
arousing. What was arousing, to me,
for three decades, was faithfulness, the
chains of orgasms extreme beyond violent
in safety. This morning, each snowflake is made of
50 or 100 or 1,000 snowflakes
roughly welded together. I sit on the
windowsill, and look up at the falling
nests and bassinets—wheelbarrows
of snow, duvets and tulles, a falcon
of snow,
a buteo,
a mouse shirt of snow, an aggregate flake
the size of a hand a month before birth,
matzohs of snow, easter baskets,
gel petals
moving slowly
up and sideways in the heavy buoyant
solution of the air. Once, during a
thunderstorm on the mountain, I lay
in the torrent, on my back, on the big stone
in front of Galway's front door,

and the swollen, ash, pork belly, teated
clouds came lower and lower in the hail,
until they seemed just yards above me,
till Galway   put his head out   and called
"There might be lightning, pretty soon,"
and I went indoors. It was the only time I'd
taken a risk, except for when
I slept with a man for the first time—
without protection—and a lifetime later with a
promiscuous man, without a condom,
as if the only fire I would play with
was my life, or my child's life.

Cervix Aria

When I held a snapdragon gently by its jaws
and squeezed, so they opened, it was as if
the volt at the hinge of the maw of the blossom leaped
open at the same instant as the *glug!*
at the core of my body. I had no idea it was
the cervix *swallowing*, practicing for when it would
take in fresh seed, once I was grown up,
to speed to its queen, up the corridor,
in the dark.
Sometimes I wore—on my flat, ridged
chest, over the thin skin
and the latticework of my xylophonic
ribs—a smocked dress, *smock*
from *(s)meugh,* "slippery, to slip, to slip on >
see: SMUGGLE, MEEK, *MUCUS.*" I forget
how the body first appeared on earth, was it in
drifts, like a cloud of milkweed seed, then
flesh, which longed to make more of itself,
and without knowing how, was able to.
We almost knew this, at five, four,
three—when we saw the truth of beauty,
our body, abashed, gulped.

Calabash Aria

And when it was my turn, I went up on the stage,
to speak from within the world Adjoa
and Christina and Colson and Ishion and Russell
had set us further and further into—
our own souls. So I sang to them, and to
Kwame, who had brought us here
from around the island and the world—I could almost
feel the unimaginable size of the
earth under my feet—and then
I did my ditties, honor to the tee-tees
and ta-tas, and when I finished one,
the great calabash basin of the hearers
tilted up and gave me golden
sound to drink. Then I sawed my little
fiddle-arm again, and they seed what I sawed,
and sang me back—seesaw, we poured
light back and forth between us. And then,
near the end of my time—I was about to give what I had
made of what my mother had given me, the
beatings, and the music—I felt
the full bowl of us, in the tent,
and felt, behind me, the sea, and the night, and the
oval platter of our solar home,
and the constellations beyond it, in which we
glimpse our stories, and I felt the great
sash of the Milky Way, as if we are
resting on our own shoulders, and then
I sang my mother out—I sang
the mothers and fathers out, into the stars
and the nothing beyond them, into which we will
follow them, at the end of our turn.

California Aria

I loved the shape
of my home state,
jackknifed to the east,
its navel a lake,
its chest a vertical plane, its abdomen
a slope of one hundred and forty degrees
off vertical, its waist a lean
teenage stomach's concave angle, its
front geometrical,
its curved back coastal with inlets and
outlets. I was proud of my Golden State,
and when, in 1958, the no
makeup came
along, and the no
underwear, and the no comb, and the
all-black clothing, it was O.K.
for me to be no lady, like my state
with the round heels—falling over
backwards, into the Pacific, and riven with
stream and creek splits like the sharp
sexual feelings which ran through us. Now,
I'm learning there was no California
until recently, we arrived late,
riding the ocean floor in
from the mid-sea trench the magma boiled out of,
until we collided with the shore of Nevada
and pushed the Sierra up. I loved
the bent-handle shape of my state,
the L of it, the crooked C,
and the way it made a curly edge for the
continent. But since 1953,
when I saw the mask of blood of a fallen-down-
drunk right-wing Republican
covering my father's face, I have hated
scarlet, and since November 8,
2016, I have been sad to hate
my native shape, the dihedral edge
of my tectonic plate—my stolen, my blue Red State.

Departure Gate Aria

She was standing near a departure gate,
sandal-footed, her wiggly hair
and the latticework of her mercury footwear
the same satiny gold, and there was something
wistful about her, under the burnish
of her makeup she looked extremely young,
and a little afraid. I wanted to speak
to her, as if I were a guardian spirit
working the airport—God knows
I was crazed with my fresh solitariness—
so I did a little double take,
when I passed her, and said, Could I ask, where did you
get your sandals—my husband, I lied,
wants me to get some, and she said a name, as if
relieved to speak. Thanks, I said,
they look great with your hair—actually
(my head bowed down on its own), you look
like a goddess. Her face came out from behind
its cloud, You don't know how I needed that!,
she cried out, I'm going to meet my boyfriend's
parents. You'll do just fine, I said, you look
beautiful and good. She looked joyful. I bustled off—
so this is what I'll do, now,
instead of kissing and being kissed, I'll
go through airports praising people, like an
Antichrist saying, You do not need
to change your life.

Early Pastoral Aria

I did not push my baby brother
in, when he fell into the swimming pool
in the woods at our father's parents', I was nowhere
near him, he was singing to the baby
on the surface of the water, who was singing to him when he
tipped over, and went in, as if back
into the sky from which he had descended on the
last day that I was my mother's
baby. They say he went straight to the bottom
of the handmade clay pool, and when my
mother got to the edge he was lying near the
drain, smiling. She dove in,
in her clothes, like a bird in its feathers, I wish I had
seen that
Olympus moment
in my mom's life, she brought him and his
smile up into the air again.
Sometimes that pool was dry, like a pit
a child might be put in, like the one Joseph
was put in, when they took from him
his coat of many colors, the most
beautiful thing in the world, like being
your mother's baby—you were magic, then,
and not again. And something took him
and threw him back where he had come from, and she dove
from heaven into the deep to recover
her heart's desire. Then the pool was drained,
no more guppying about, like a tailless
boy, a pole-less tad, but just
the mountain sun, around the baked
and cracking rim, with clay ducks
hissing with dryness, and if you were invited you could
go into the bush of thorns
and find a massive blackberry and
put it in your mouth and slowly crush it,
all for yourself, your solitary
voluptuous mouth.

Fear of Motherhood Aria

For months, something had pulled back, in me,
as if into hiding. There was a being
growing inside me, larger and larger, who would
have to come out, through the delicate passage.
Something in me backed up in terror
from that. And when the pain of birthing seemed to
tear the center of my center, something
tried to flatten its back as if
against the back wall of some closet in some
anti-immolative chamber. But then
she was here, so slight, so touching. But when
the milk came in, and my breasts hardened,
something deep in me wanted to withdraw,
inward, further. And one of my milk spouts
cracked and split, and I fed our beauty
through a rubber shield, and the other cracked,
and that thing inside me drew back and held its breath.
I would look down on the river-delta,
the silver and pearl of the stretch-marks
on the wine-skins, and I was glad it worked,
but something in me did not join in,
as if I wanted to save some freedom
or humanness from female animalness,
from motherness. This lasted until she was a
few weeks, then the something which had
pressed back against some back wall
and sucked in its gut to try to back further
in hopes of being passed over, began
to breathe again, and slowly came
the sweet routine, and the very small child
began to smile, and sing, and over
time the soul of the young mother
came further and further from the sense of near-death
and dissolution, she came forward, almost
fully, into her new life, and
what had been ripped

out was filled
in, muscle with scar tissue sparkle. But she
did not forget she had seen through
her life, into her nature. When she helped
a tiny arm into a sleeve—
or cooked, or bathed, or nursed—she loved,
but this had been not only love,
it had been like swimming in a flood, treading water
to stay up, live or die. Live,
and die.

Global Aria

First I stuck the pitchfork in, then I
stepped up onto the base of the tines,
both sides, and jumped—hard-
candy christmas. Then I pulled
the long, wooden shaft down toward me, then I
jumped on the red steel handle. Fountain
of dirt! And when I had a four-tine
dotted line
around the rim
of a circle, I shoveled the earth out
in four piles. Rain, sun, the
rocks now pale gray. Then,
pogo stick of the fork again,
a deeper layer, with underground
earthworm rainbows in subtle penis
colors—gather each up in a fistful of
humus and cache them in safety—handsome
collars and bright nice ridges of face
glans or foreskin. Then comb-hair and coffee grounds
and eggshells go in, then the worms go back,
the topsoil goes back, and my boots, with twenty
pounds of rich
loam on each,
stamp the earth down.
Add an old window screen, with some
old bricks on it, and a black
plastic garbage bag with its long
scarlet tongue hanging out,
and a quartzite zinc bucket upside
down on top. Sleep, baby,
sleep, the winter snow will be deep.
In spring I will turn the ground and plant
my mother's bush, and from it raise
a pair of breasts to feed a nation,
a planet of water, a blue hydrangea.

Gliss Aria

In the tub, buoyant, a creature moving through
very heavy air, barely flying,
soaring in place, washing my once-
nameless, my secret-named place, my
Between-Your-Legs, I thank the inner
lining of my inner lips
for keeping its pure gliss decade after
decade, century after century,
as if I am iconic, a fountain
whose waters are fresh, era after
geological era, as if
my lips are not merely mine, but have seemed to
belong, some hours,
to a man, to a child,
to my species. And I have not, always,
treated them well, I have sat on them and
sat on them, for hours, in summer
heat, sometimes I have left them untouched,
so they cannot sing, yet they've been sweet to me,
liquidy, sleek, lissome, with some
faint fragrance of salted nectar.
Other parts of my body have worn
out, worn down, been ground away, dried
up (though one
breast still makes,
once a moon, one drop of cream),
but the kissing lips of life, the inner
sheath of the mouth of ecstasy
remains as silver-pale-green as the wet
deeps of a cactus which guardians us in the
fierce desert—the core of our being, the slake.

Graduation Aria

When she'd tried to shush the families behind us,
and in front of us, and beside us, scowling
in fastidious distaste—they were *chatting*, during
her grandson's graduation—when
the ceremony had ended; when the dinner
was eaten, when we took her back
to her room in the college dormitory like a
medieval fortress, and went
over the room, with her, again—
the window, the light, the heat, the key,
the bathroom she would share with strangers—
I pretended everything was fine, but I saw
for a moment that my mother really had been
an orphan, she'd never for a moment had a mother
who could love her. So I kissed her forehead, and left her
there, little pack-rat in an old stone room
with a twenty-four-foot ceiling, and I went
upstairs, and in a narrow dorm bed like a
trough my husband and I flew through the
air caroling—now I see I was
trilling like the wren who threw the phoebe
nestling out of the back-porch nest, I was
that kind of happy, having put
my mother in durance. For years, then,
I ate my gladness of her anxious night
without knowing I was eating it.
Weeks before her death, she smiled, and
said, "Remember that dungeon?" and I kissed her
with sudden affection toward the one who without
having been loved by her own mother
had taught me to love her and hate her, to hate and love.

Hyacinth Aria

When my mother was felled, by the sudden blow
of a stroke, decked by a deep bleed when the old
brain tumor broke through, and I flew
to her, and sang to her for the rest
of her life, for two days, sang her
out, they told my students where I'd
been, and there on the seminar table
was a garden, in a small shoebox
crate, with a lattice, wooden fence, in-
side it the spears of hyacinths.
This morning I leaned over her cut-glass bowl so
cut it looks about to draw blood,
and there in the water jellied with peeling
bulb-skin, down inside the thighs of the shoots there was a
cunning jumble of bumps, rinds,
green mother grinds of hyacinths
soon to bulge and rise and open,
and, for a moment, I almost mourned
my mother—mourned her when she was a child,
a frail being like an insect, with papery
wings, with little, veined skirts,
before she had pummeled anyone,
before she had taken the cudgel from her own
mother to wield it in turn on me who would
take it in turn as my purple stylus,
my gold pen. And so, for a moment,
I loved my mother—she was my first chance,
my last chance, to love the human.

Immigration Aria

I bring you a tired song of my poor
femur-knob. I huddled in my chair before
I walked—the leg weighs twice the other, I
swing its masses of fluid along like an
enclosed falls. My mother's people
came here yearning to sing to their God,
to breathe free, men and women
attacked by their landlords, who called them wretched
refuse, teeming with vermin. They'd pushed off from that
shore, homeless on the ocean, through calm
and tempest—sometimes in sight of a fountain
tossed up out of the brow of a fish—until
they came to these low hills which lift up from a
land where we have set a lamp
with a golden torch, to remind us, here
at the door: entering through it is a promise
to leave it open behind us.

Jockey Aria

Suddenly, I remember them—
can it be a year since I have seen them, my ex-first-
post-divorce-boyfriend's underpants—
especially the royal-blue ones,
and the starless, moonless, midnight black,
and the valentine red, those cartoon swells
of the heart. I loved them on him, I loved them part
off—drawn like the bowstring, or grasped
like the bow's sinewy handle. And the sight of them
later, in the still dark, fallen
on the field, gave joy of the necessary
wreckage of the mortal casings
of eros. I have liked to live in the
proximity of male underpants,
a shy honor, as if I were partway
admitted into the temple of the other,
but his, I adored with a golden calf
idolatry, as if to be close to a
man were everything, to some nothing
in me, and as if the belling of the weave, in its
worn give, gave me some proof of
familiarness, and loyalty,
and staying power, and tenderness,
and intimate substantialness,
all in the bright tints of a self
celebrating itself, the male
girding his loins in beauty. The memory
brings me to my knees, not just with desire, though with a
calf's lowing desire, but with my old
false ideas—that he owned himself,
with a closed, owning dignity,
and I did not own myself, and I wanted to feel
owned by him. God help me. How do I
shine, in my own eyes, as my ex-
boyfriend's sacred underpants shine?
I ask you! And I know, I know, when it comes to the
haunting, self-preening beauty of the other,
I have to ask my mother.

Kunitzeiform Aria

Did you know T. S. Eliot wore eyeshadow,
sometimes, I asked Stanley, and he chuckled—one
gurgle in the bubble chamber
of the spirit level—and his eyes had that sensual
brightness, and his big, fleshless, elegant
hand lifted, and soared over, and dropped,
a couple of times, on the back of my hand, like
being patted by matter. *I didn't*
know that, he musicaled up.
Someone said he'd dust his lids
with green, so someone would say, "Are you
O.K., Tom, and Stanley said,
It's a hard way to go about doing that,
and I rubbed the heel of my hand over the rough
nest-material of Stanley's tweed
sleeve, and said, *You have a generous heart, I*
sometimes laugh at Eliot for that, like some
kind of revenge on his politics—
what about you, Stanley, what were your
feelings about him? And Stanley
drew on time, and space, he drew on
his powers, and their sleep, and their dreams, he worked,
like God not resting on the sixth day,
and then, when his thought was done, he turned his
long, loping engine toward the task
of telling it, word by word. He said, *I was,*
and paused—I love to pause with him, on the
long boat, our hands trailing in the
water of a hundred years—*I was,*
pause, pause, we breathe in,
we breathe out, *I was fortunate*
in my marriage, he said, and we went, again,
out into the empyrean
of quiet, beyond the atmosphere,
overboard, and then the return,
and then the refrain, *I was fortunate,*

I think, and I rubbed his invisible weaving
with my thumb, and said, *You were, you were—*
you loved and were loved. He nodded, his arms and
body still, he wondered as he wandered,
out under the sky, *I was fortunate*
in my marriages, I think, he said,
But still, there was all that sorrow, he turned his
face to me, I petted the wool like a
stanch made of spider wodge with some
roots and twigs in it, over his
forearm, he looked into my eyes with that stalwart look,
I put my hand on the mastodon
of his buoyant hand, which was resting, now,
as a swimmer at the end of a stroke may glide,
may glide, desire, desire, rest,
desire. When I
had let myself in,
he'd been facing the other way, signing
books, and I had put the huge
stargazer lily over his shoulder, like
a horse looking over a stall gate, and he'd
turned and seen it, in surprise and pleasure, and
recognized it, and took its head in his
hands and softly rubbed its five ears.

Long-Playing Aria

Years after the sound-system dies of old
age—one Easter Island speaker,
then the other, then the turntable neck,
with the penny scotch-taped to the back of its head—
I got fresh stereo things, for my 1940s
78s, and my 1950s
45s, and my 1960s
33s, and was afraid to listen,
as if I might then wake up back then, and would
not have found the life I found.
But there was an album cover of a strong
grass green, a queen's robe color,
queen of cold summer, a record made in
'52, with a drawing of the new
variable groove, which left more than the
necessary land, and made use of this ordinarily
wasted land. But when I pushed the button,
and the crane swung over, my hands gripped
my head—it was as if I was hearing
the sounds of my first home, not the one
before I was born, but the one before I was
conceived. It was gorgeously orderly
and painful. It was not healing—it hurt
to hear how much healing had been needed. And it was
loving, it came out of kind, sensual
sweetness. I could feel my face, terrible, some
deep, Hebrew letter of hot Old
Testament lead, sunk in
between my brows. The joy of the music took
the measure of the wound—as if I had been loved,
or what I took for loved, before
I spoke, before words—in these chords were those earliest
days. At first, it seemed to be like hearing
the voice of the most loved, who has been lost, like
Forrest hearing Carolyn's voice.
And the green cover had holy pagan

words on it—Prades, Schubert,
Quintet, Casals, Isaac Stern—
I had played and played it, every day,
15, 16, 17, I'd
carried a stack of these cardboard squares when I
went—my body which had hardly been touched,
even through my clothes—to be that passive
verb, with *flowered* in it, by a light-shedding
laughing man who seemed to not love
anyone, like a god. And now
I could hear the music think, as I
had heard it then, the unspooling of the
logic of being mortal—of dying,
as my best friend had, when I was nine, and my
beloved, when I was sixteen. I heard,
again, what loving and being loved might
sound like—or I heard what some comfort for
the loss of that might sound like. I heard
the body and soul of death—of love
and death. It was all we had, and it would have to be enough.

Mortal Aria

(for Carl)

I don't feel that I'm slowly dying,
though I am. Many cells inside
my ears, in the ossicle, and malleus, cochlea,
have died where they lived and worked—I don't know if they're
there, still, looking like themselves
but dead, or if their corpses wore
away, broke down to their elements and were
shuffled off by capillaries,
I don't know if I peed them out
and now they're in an ocean bay
or trench, or if I breathed them out, I might
breathe one in again. And maybe
a third of the nerves in the soles of my feet
died slowly as the bones of my lumbar
backbone collapsed onto each other over
time, flattening the spinal cord.
Years ago, when the cancer had spread
in my lover's body, it appeared on the X-ray as
areas of darkness in his clavicle,
and hip, and skull. When the doctor showed us
the X-ray, I moved close to my love, so my
left arm
lay against
his right arm, that he not be without
touch, seeing that invader: *karkar:*
hard hard. It was not
an animal, or a vegetable, but
alive. It lives in him still. And they are
nuking it, which is giving him
some time. If the cancer kills him, I don't
know if it will outlive him by an hour,
or a day, before it dies. If it were not
a stupid wish, I would wish the dead
cancer could be taken out of

his body before he is dressed in a linen
shroud, I would help dress him in it.
We will sit with him, we will sing to him, he will be
put to bed in the earth he loves.
I think of him at four years old in the
little three-piece suit and cap
his parents dressed him and his brother in,
a look of amazement, wonder, almost
bafflement on his beautiful face.
Off and on, all his life, he has
emitted light. I would watch him sleep
in the dark woods, his brow reflecting starlight.

Morning Aria, 6,000 Feet

First I clean the hotel room hot plate
so I will not smell any burnt once-living matter,
washing the metal and checking the paper towel,
as when, after I shit, I wipe
and look, to see if it's clean, that almost
unknown floral knob back down there in prehistory.
Then, I untangle the machine's cord, which is
bent, flattened, crinkled, crushed
like my spinal cord on the X-ray, silver
snake caught between the boulders of a collapsed stone wall.
The coffee filling the pot looks beautiful this morning,
made from mountain water,
then I realize I had forgotten to put any ground beans in,
and I start over. I am starting over.
I am laying down my ambition—to disguise that I am a creature of
      narcissus,
as if a daughter of narcissus could be anything but a narcissus.
I am not seeking a man to love and be loved by,
though of course I always am,
I am asking to learn to like this large awkward being,
flightless dragon damsel fly—
Fashion thyself, then others shall thee beare—
to pull up my vanity, out of the backyard dirt,
where I buried it when I saw that it and I could not both go forth
      alive from that house.
Yesterday morning, I woke in an aquarium
of heavy, monoxide, sea-level, Bay air.
This morning I woke in an aerie with very little oxygen in it.
And I am so old now!
Dear old one, I could learn to care for you.
I like the worn scar of your first titanium hip,
barely visible by now on the choppy sea of your posterior,
I even like the fresh anterior scar
across your inguinal fold, completing
a fierce X. I said I was tired
of loving my mother and father—I was so
vain about being able to love them.
But who says I love them? If I loved them, I could love myself.

Nevada City, Calif., Aria

When I sit up from sleep and swing my legs over the side of the flat
        world,
then push down with my palms to heave my weight up,
the bed makes a cry, not like an animal, not like a person,
but like metal being taken from its underground home,
the spiral torque of an iron spring.
It isn't true I was ever anything like an eland.
My young (I use you again here easily, my dearest ones,
as if I have no respect for human rights)
did not nurse standing up on four legs, did not tup
from a soft leather gourd between ungulate hind legs,
though I had been a leaper, back when my body took
shapes like drifts of mist above a pond fed by a
narrow long waterfall.
I can hardly believe that dancer's willow ripple was my torso,
and I felt at home in it, I could bear its beauty,
and I knew I was born to lie down in it in a woods with another
        person.
Now the heavy flesh of the years of misdirected love is beginning to
        come off,
I am lopping it—rich queen rinds and collops of fat.
I am desperate to love myself, to tolerate myself,
vanity mixed in with it is fine, pride is fine, all avails.
Others who hate injustice and extermination and murder
are willing to go into these intimate places,
a stadium of blood and excrement,
to hate it directly, up close, inches from it, touching it.
When I am at my lowest, do I hate myself?
I suspect her and have contempt for her.
And except for my friends—when I'm low, do I hate everyone?
I hate the sun, which I can feel broiling my exposed surfaces.
I hate the wind, which tickles me with my own hair-tips to arouse
        and madden me.
But I do not hate these old curtains in this old hotel room.
I love that they cannot move toward me on their own and hurt me.
I love that they are made of cotton lace,

I love the background scrim like thousands of tiny bee sexagons,
and the images of pelmets and swags on one curtain,
and on another, roses bulging to open,
and pineapple in succulent conifer armor,
and another with a delicate crosshatch background,
flattened lace bows with wrinkled loops and corkscrew ties,
and small shields stippled with seed-pods like a lady's escutcheon.
And I love my *parea*, translucent, black with white flowers,
which I draped over the dark mirror of the television screen,
moving one scree swallowtail volute at the edge
to cover the red light which means always on,
the light which means because we hate ourselves
we are igniting the earth.

Object Permanence Aria

What a moment it was, in my life, when my mother
would leave the room, and I knew she still
existed! I was connected to that giant
flower on legs, that huge human
bee, even when the evidence of her
was invisible to me. Maybe she'd been singing,
when she'd walked out, through the door,
the portal to non-existence, and her singing
came back to me from some world beyond
this life, my brain adding thousands of fresh
cells to itself, every hour.
And now I remember my elder sister, my
emissary of sanity,
maybe she taught me object constancy,
her head below the level of my crib
mattress where I lay, helpless ruler
up on my cloud. She would give me things,
through the bars, and her solemn face and her night-black
eyes would watch what I did. I was her little
warm-blooded aquarium dweller,
slowly pulling my amphibian self
up onto dry land. But I think it was
the big, electric one, the apron
manta ray, in relation to whom
I surmised the hall in which she moved like
Revelations toward my sill.
And when, in the morning, from her own cage,
my sister would call for our mother, soon I
would call for her too, and our mother would call
back to us—that was the song
of my early life, each of us
blind to each other and to the future, singing together.

Pasadena Aria

1

When I drove into your home town,
for the first time, a big pine-cone
hurtled down in front of the hood!
I parked and retrieved it, the stomen tip
green and wet. An hour later,
I realized that you had never once
thrown anything at me. And, as days
passed, the Ponderosa oval
opened, its bracts stretched apart,
and their pairs of wings on top dried
and lifted. Thank you for every spoon,
and fork, and knife, and saucer, and cup.
Thank you for keeping the air between us
kempt, empty, aeolian.
Never a stick, or a perfume bottle,
or pinking shears—as if you were saving
an inheritance of untainted objects to
pass down to me. You know why I'm still
writing you, don't you. I miss you, as I have
ever since nine months after I was born,
when you first threw something at me while keeping
hold of it—then threw it again,
and again and again—when you can throw the same thing
over and over, it's as if you have
a magic power, an always replenishable
instrument. Of course if you had let
go of the big beaver-tail hairbrush—
if it had been aimed at my head—I would have
had it. I'm letting you have it, here,
casting a line out, to catch you, then
coming back, then casting one out,
to bind you to me, flinging this flurry of
make-a-wish milkweed.

2

When I sleep for the first time in the town
where my mother was a child, a spider climbs up
into the bathtub before first light.
I bag it and find a cherry tree, and step
within its branches, like the many-corsaged
arms of a dancer, I open and up-
end the bag, and the creature floats down
out of it on her self-expression,
her scarce-visible thread. I wind it
around a blossom, and she legs it up
between the layered petticoats.
Bending toward the ground, I peer toward the sky, I feel
happy looking up my mother's young
multiple skirts, as if I am
an innocent, and a search into her inmost
nature is allowed. Her abdomen
is black with white spots, her thorax dark golden,
her maxillary palps steadily moving
as if in a creek's current. I am looking
up, into the hidden, again,
head back, where a bird I cannot
discern, sings. And I panic, a little,
for my mother, I want to say: Remember,
I never understood her—in a way,
I never knew her. All morning I am glad
to think of the arachnid, hunting
on her own terms, inside the moist
crinolines of the arboreal flowers,
far from me, free of me,
alive, unseen.

Pugilist Aria

When I am reading about boxing, I wish
I could have faced my mother, in the ring, when we were
roughly the same height, same weight,
in between the time she was still
taller than I, and when I was finally
taller than she. O if Jesus and God and the
Neuter Ghost had said to us We want you to
fight full out. I can see my mom
with abs, with biceps, her permanent wave
hair held back in a fillet like Wonder Woman's,
she 38, and I 12, she would
not have stood a chance, I was so much
madder at her than she at me—she had
beaten me since I was what, a year
old? O let me shine horrific,
fur-ballistic, in the costume I wore to
Spring Day, at 13, not knowing any better,
a girl loin-cloth/chest-cloth and a club and
hair teased out into fright fur
with backyard dirt. I don't know if I
could do it, actually—aim my
right hook at my mother's little
glass jaw, and follow through,
reckless to express myself,
Mary and God and the Holy Spirit
egging me on, and there to protect her—I could
hit her with *all my strength*, and I would not kill her.

Q Aria

Q belonged to Q & A,
to questions, and to foursomes, and fractions,
it belonged to the Queen, to Quakers, to quintets—
within its compound in the dictionary dwelt
the quill pig, and quince beetle,
and quetzal, and quail. Quailing was part of *Q*'s
quiddity—the *Q* quaked
and quivered, it quarreled and quashed. No one was
quite sure where it had come from, but it had
traveled with the *K*, they were the two voiceless
velar Semitic consonants, they went
back to the desert, to *caph* and *koph*.
And *K* has done a lot better—
28 pages in Webster's Third
to *Q*'s 18. And though *Q* has much
to be proud of, from *Q & I detector*
through *quinoa*, sometimes these days the letter
looks like what medical students called the
Q face—its tongue lolling out.
And sometimes when you pass a folded
newspaper, you can hear from within it
a keening, from all the *Q*s who are being
set in type, warboarded,
made to tell and tell of the quick and the
Iraq dead.

Rasputin Aria

I wish I did not think of Rasputin
so often. To have been born with a penis which in
manhood would be said to be,
erect, 14" long,
some said 18",
organ which he used in brutal
acts, penetrating helplessness,
and then, at the end of his life, to be taken
from behind, raped, then castrated,
penis and testicles, harps of the nerves,
gone—and then to be killed one way,
and it did not take, and then another,
then stabbed and drowned in a sack—
though all that was found was the skein of burlap
bitten and torn open and washed up—
a cruel male leader, a brigand,
law unto himself, taken, the shock of it, the
disbelief, the poor anus from the
worldwide family of anuses,
the species' helpless O, and the poor
penis, brother to the poor sister
vagina—'tis of thee I think
when I think of my country rendering,
and being rendered, when I think of our body
politic, its head of wrath
and flame face, and swamp-gas hair.

Sepia Aria

In the pictures when my father was a young man,
he is standing alone. His own father,
his eyes glittering, is standing with my father's
sister, holding her close, and she is staring,
as if the surface of her face is liquid—
incredulous panic. And my father's mother stands
alone, her face grim. And the son—
two heads taller than his parents—looks baffled,
distraught. As a child, he'd peered at the camera, as if
trying to see
into it,
to its engineering—his head cocked,
his eye bright as a Bewick wren's.
He never learned to read and write
too well, block printed his way through college
into the corporation and the private
scenes of adult life. As a child
he was wild with eagerness, but by
the year he was the tallest in his family
he could not tell what was going on,
the flesh of his forehead twisted with invisible
tongs, he stands there balked, stymied,
handsome—he looks as if, at any
moment, if he could, he would burst into anguished song.

Silver Spoon Aria

I was born with a silver spoon in my mouth,
and a silver knife, and a silver fork.
I would complain about it—the spoon was not greasy,
it tasted like braces, my shining access
to cosmetic enhancement. And I complained about
the taste of my fillings in my very expensive
mouth, as if only my family was paying—
where did I think the rich got
their money but from everyone else?
My mother beat me in 4/4 time,
and I rant, now, to her beat—I wear
her rings as if I killed her for them, as my
people killed, and climbed up over
our dead. And I sound as if I am bragging
about it. I was born with a spoon instead of a
tongue in my mouth—dung spoon,
diamond spoon. And who would I be
to ask for forgiveness? I would be a white girl.
And I hear Miss Lucille, as if on the mountain
where I'd stand beside her, and brush away insects,
and sometimes pick one off her, sometimes
by the wings, and toss it away. And Lucille
is saying, to me, You have asked for enough,
and been given to in excess. And that thing in your mouth,
open your mouth and let that thing go,
let it fly back into the mine where it was brought
up from the underworld, at the price of
lives, beloved lives. And now,
enough, Shar, now a decent silence.

Scansion Aria

When I'm think / ing a bout / scansion,
weak-weak-STRONG, weak-weak-STRONG, STRONG-weak,
ana*pest*, ana*pest*, *trochee*—
if I want to know a poem, Biblically,
respiratorily, cardio-
vascularly, I chart the rhythms
of its lines—and I no longer fear that beat
interests me so deeply because I was a
child beaten to the 4/4 beat
of the hymns. I love scansion because it is related
to *dansion*—it gets to know the *action*
of the poem in order to know its passion.
And what if I was not passive,
all those years, obeying the command
to go upstairs, and strip to the waist
from the floor up, the garments in any
order—as if one would ever not
leave the underpants to last,
covering one's core, though I did not know there was a
passageway, inside me, I knew
only the soft beak, in which
the gorgeous music played, sometimes.
Not then, standing on her rug, like the earth
in the old model of the universe,
or the parent in the brain of the child—and wait, ten
minutes, an hour . . . What if I was
receiving not just destruction, when she beat me, but
clenching myself, hard, around
my soul, to protect it? What if I
was a warrior—what if I won?! Here
we are, after all, singing to each other,
taking turns
being the baby,
being the mother,
/ - - / -   ,, / - - / - ,
dactyl, trochee, dactyl, trochee,
active witness, active witness of the witness.

Scrapbook Aria

In the old photo, we are sitting, my sister
upright, like a falls—her bridalveil spine,
the ferro plumbline of her hair—and I,
I hunched over, tongue sticking out,
jaws working like a pair of kindergarten
scissors. The black, fibrous scrapbook
pages were sooty, the catalogs
shiny, the library paste was in a crockery
pot. There were rich children in fancy
underwear, to cut out, there were ladies
in huge, monkey-brain hats, there were Victorian
mothers and babies. I ate the paste
like wintergreen birthday-cake frosting. My sister,
still taller than I, had existed since before
I was born, and whatever she was wearing, as we sat,
I would be wearing, in about six months—
and though she could do everything better, I was
starting to catch up. After our mother
died, fifty years later, we sat
on her floor, like this, and divvied up
the spoils, with what we both felt
was perfect fairness. On those long-ago days we had
not yet known to take turns, choosing first—
of course the firstborn, then, chose first, though
sometimes, if I groaned or sighed,
she couldn't resist, but hand over
some image of a pretty young mother.
Long gone, to brittle dried
mucilage, and fractured ancient
paper, the albums—and enduring the length of our
lives the sense of being one
of two, half of a wholehearted love.

Timothy Aria

Until I was fully born—even while my
crown was moving toward the surface of my mother, then
was framed in her nether rock-star hair—
I was Timothy. I'd been Timothy
for nine months, and I was Timothy
when the sexual palm of her body passed up
over my brow, and nose, and mouth,
and chin, in the motion which is opposite
to the closing of the dead's eyelids,
my boy face bathed in the last
air which as Timothy I'd breathe. In my handsome
mask of him, I was breathing in through the
umbilical artery, taking my last
air as a guy, direct from her, and
breathing out, into her—
exhaust goddess—through my umbilical
vein. And I rotated, to the side,
as Timothy, never to be Timmy,
oval of my shoulders to the oval of her portal,
until my head was out in the room,
and I paused, a moment, perfect in
her eyes, in the delivery-room mirror
down there, framed in stainless steel,
the royal portrait of her son, my penis—
Timothy's penis, in a way still
my mother's penis—still hidden.
So it's not as if I never had
a life as a man. And I do like
to pause, here, in my liquid gender,
till the gush, the last
rush. And was
the first song I heard from my mother
a disappointed moan? And if my father had been
in that room, would I have heard a sigh
of relief, from him? And I tore my first
puzzle piece of breath out of the

sky—which I have yet to return—
and I sang my first note, my wail,
and the pink in my faintly bluish body
bloomed. And then, I rested, as actors
rest, between parts. But I had been a star,
for a while, and I did not forget that I'd been
held, once, at some length, in passionate regard.

Tailbone Aria

It's been happening since the day after
the colonoscopy, when the natty
physician, in violet tie, said, Turn on your
left side, and I started to count
down from 100. All was normal,
and the next day, when I had shittened
and wiped, once twice Puritan thrice,
I actually reached around and touched
my own tailbone, there at my center of
gravity, near the sacral
ganglion, then down along the coccyx, its
strong dis-graduated necklace
of monkey pearls. It was as if
I wanted to see what the doc had seen,
what I had seen, on babies I had changed,
what I had kissed on my few lovers, like the
hinge of a butterfly between
the plush, luscious wings. I was
afraid—I'd heard that love had pitched
its tent in the place of excrement—
but day by day I got used to it,
the soft skin on the other side of the
world, the obturator externus
muscles, the levator ani, left
and right, the dimple between. It was like
making peace with the ancient cere-
bellum, at the base of the nape,
the reptile brain. I did not want to
venture as far as the gathers and folds
of the asshole, but just to pet the abstract
sculptural principles, above it,
like a child at a petting zoo, or a grown-up
on the back side of the moon for a moment—
or like myself, as a child, if I had
known how to be at home with myself, to make
peace with my sweet body.

Uncombed Aria

When I did not comb my hair for a week—
a foot and a half long—elder
maenad, I would twist my hanks
into will-o'-the-wisps, I would braid my locks and wear
crowns of them. I would wash it, matted,
and let it come out matted and shining,
and braid the snaggles, but then I began
to step, one finger at a time, onto the pocked
forest floor atop my scalp,
atop my skullcap's rock—walk,
walk, vines grown together,
root systems twined—walk, pull
gently, pop of a follicle coming
out, oval translucent cork,
walk. Spiders also have 8
fingers, one on each of their 8 hands
which are feet. When one repairs a web, does she
first pick free the wadded threads
or does she mush the mishmash together like the
signature of the *Argiope?*
An hour, at the loom, the left hand
the woof, the right the slow un-warp,
the bowl of the sink mounded with a gray
nimbus cloud, I scoop it up
and loop and spiral it until I have
a skein like a nest. I drop it in the carton with the
coffee grounds—the acid of
the keratin will go, with them, and with
the snapper pond silt, into
the hole dug for a hydrangea plant—
milk of my mother's body to blossoms of her
dream breasts—blue dust
to dust, the human blues of the mother's breast.

Vermont Aria

At the end of the day, at the end of the evening,
in full night, I finally turn out
the light and go to one of your dormer
windows—the eaves pulled down, over
my shoulders, as if I am out over
the hollyhocks and the barrel of nasturtiums, the
flowers with their divinity in their
throats to be sucked out, the deep
panes set into the roof, the house set
halfway up the hill on top of the
mountain over the valley. We are most of the
way up to the zenith, the clouds
stretching out, level with us,
rumpled, bunched, ruched, as if we are
upside down, as if the sky
is the element we are floating on, like
liquid, as if we're at the bottom of the earth,
resting on the ocean of the air and its wrack of
glisteny seaweed and kelp. The summer
screen mesh
makes the sexagonal
hivation of the atmosphere visible,
the honeycombage of the lower heavens,
the trees are black, the grass is gray, like a
painting of an alpen mountainside
in moonlight. By day in the house now, laughter,
and the dogs' laughs and harks; by night,
the skies flow
over the slopes,
fireflies flash with frugal economy
here and there on the ground—and tiny
silver pieces of the storm are caught in the
woven metal which billows like tethered
cloth. Hello, dear Galway. Off and
on, all day, dark purple
and deluge, so I've not yet waded up the last

slant of the Northeast Kingdom—before it
falls off into the Van Allen and Orion
belts—to stand, my bones assembled
roughly upright in their constellation
above yours
now edged a little
here and there—inched—by the creatures
with whom you share the dirt and share
your tissue, drifting through their noisome jaws
in lacy jags. I am honored to be here,
almost at home in your blood's and heart's
tribe, though having little right,
neither daughter nor lover, subbeing
of the same sub species, the eaters of our words, and of
each other's, and singers of them, we cannot
keep a line
down for long, but must
throw it up, out of us,
for song, and in the middle of the night, as I
sleep with my mouth open, your music
sieves out onto the pillowcase,
seeping sweets like a hive, O great
bee on the mountain, we sing you and we celebrate you.

Waist Aria

There were lots of waists in the Bible—*the waist*
howling wilderness, the boar
who dost waist the vine, and *the waist places*
of the fat ones, and *thy waist and thy desolate*
and ruined places. And it was in an onionskin
book, too—a waist of honor
in a lust of shame is something in action,
or something—but mostly the waists were in
my mother's command. First came *Young lady—*

and now, stop reading! Whoever has had
enough of the subject, throw the fucking
magazine across the room! We don't
need you here.

        And now that it's just
us, we can go on, to what followed
Young lady—go up and wait for me
with your clothes off, below the waist—
action that is power's lust. O hourglass,
O human figure, sign of eternity
standing up on its hind legs,
cinch-belt in junior high, girdle
of Aphrodite, O magician's dotted
saw-line, raw song of coming back
from being laid waste.

X Y Z Aria

When I was ten, this building was built—
1,340 apartments—
desecrating the neighborhood.
Ten years later, the three towers,
twice as tall, were added, across
the street, the ghosts of the roads passing
through them—
where the waters
of the melted
glaciers will rise, maybe slowly at first, up the
ankles of the high-rise stilts. Eventually I'll
launch my canoe
out my window,
when the flood gets up to 17,
and make my way to my mother and father—
taking no food, in order to get to them
sooner—to return, to them,
the last breath that each gave me
out of their mouth, to return to them
the alphabet they trusted me with.

Run Away Up

I Cannot Say I Did Not

I cannot say I did not ask
to be born. I asked with my mother's beauty,
and her money. I asked with my father's desire
for his orgasms and for my mother's money.
I asked with the cradle my sister had grown out of.
I asked with my mother's longing for a son,
I asked with patriarchy. I asked
with the milk which would well in her breasts, needing to be
drained by a little, living pump.
I asked with my sister's hand-me-downs,
lying folded. I asked with geometry, with
origami, with swimming, with sewing, with
what my mind would thirst to learn.
Before I existed, I asked, with the love of my
children, to exist, and with the love of their children.
Did I ask with my tiny flat lungs
for a long portion of breaths? Did I ask
with the space in the ground, like a portion of breath,
where my body will rest, when it is motionless,
when its elements move back into the earth?
I asked, with everything I did not
have, to be born. And nowhere in any
of it was there meaning, there was only the asking
for being, and then the being, the turn
taken. I want to say that love
is the meaning, but I think that love may be
the means, what we ask with.

Mourning Undone

I think I had almost no mourning to do
when I was just born. Maybe I missed
being held, close, in that musical night,
like someone slipped into a singer's mouth for
safekeeping, or missed the cello bowels,
the gut of horse and cat and mother—
but I almost did not know that I
was missing them, my mind a field un-
scored, a moon unfootprinted.
Causes of mourning would appear, some of them
fed as they arose, feted and sated, some
pushed aside—next to some people
something walks, like a starveling, sometimes
for a lifetime. When I think of doing the work
of my undone mourning, I think I see,
before me, in the ground, stairs appear
down into the earth—and myself, and my starveling, descending.

First Breath

As soon as she is born—she,
he—the moment the newborn breathes
for the first time, taking, from the general
supply, some air, pulling it down
half her length, into the base of the
lobe which had first existed as a mattery
idea, and then had become the folded
lung, which lay in blue wait;
as soon as the sky
is drawn in, like a
petal expanding, in fast motion,
opening into the new being—
oxygen, where it had never been,
taking the neonate's bluish shade
back into the empyrean;
as soon as she's taken the good of one breath,
and given back the rest—look,
she is dying. I mean she is living—for a time,
maybe ninety years—but she
is on her way, now, to that ending.
She had never died at all, until now,
never before been offered the human work.

The Task of Naming Me

I don't think the task of naming me
fell to my father because they knew
the sex of the child was decided by the sperm—
I don't think they knew that. They thought that giving
a name was a big deal, so it should be
a man who did it—and my mother was grieving,
her father in heaven had given her
another daughter. In the room where new parents
pay and check out, they won't let you take
your baby home if you haven't named her.
I think there would have been a flourish,
a flash for the nurses in his dark brown eyes,
a delay as he closed his eyes and held his
frat-boy finger above the open
Bible, then brought his digit down into the
creek-bed of eros, the laid-open lady book,
and touched my name.
This morning I wondered if it was on purpose
he opened the book way back in war,
in Kings and Numbers, letting the Psalms
and Proverbs and Ecclesiastes go by,
goodbye to Isaiah and Jeremiah,
and stopped, blind, at the narrow window
of a song—the slot for the crossbow's arrow
between turret bulges—he touched my name among
the roses and the lilies, I rose up
under my father's thumb, and his fruit was
sweet to my taste, and the shade of his presence
has been all my life a rich and enduring night.

My First Two Weeks,

I lived in a collective,
a commune of newborns in pink or blue blankets and
rows of plastic honeycomb cribs
on legs with wheels. That was my birth
community, on top of a hill
above the Pacific which had submarines in it—
world wartime—our attendants women
of color and of no color, and no one who was
Japanese, those neighbors had been put
in concentration camps. Every four
hours on the dot of the ward clock
they took me to my mother's breast,
I drained it in four eight-pound, full-term
gulps, and then the other breast—
I commandeered those teats! And then,
from two weeks, to three years,
I shared an apartment with my junior goddess,
my big sister, and my life god, and my
funny father, milkless, George
Lyon with his cubs—and we shared a wall with a
family with two children, twins,
Coda and Codette! Boy and girl!
Thin! Tall! White! Blond!
Six years old! And the wall had two
fireplaces, back to back,
one in their apartment, one in ours,
which shared a chimney. Before we moved,
they left—and the night before they left,
the father came after the twins with a butcher
knife, and they hid in their cold hearth,
and lived. We moved across the Bay to a house
with a shallow hearth, oiled with carbon
and ash. And our father on earth was not violent—
the time I saw him with a butcher knife in his
fist he was falling over backwards, stiff,
the blade pointed at the ceiling, like a soldier

fainting at attention—eyes open,
blind drunk. Our father in heaven
was violent, but our dad was comic—
he would laugh, in his Hawaiian shirt,
pulling at the hem of my summer shorts, he was a
fool, plumeria pistils and hibiscus
anthers and lilikoi leis, he was
an idiot, ignorant, and, for a sadist, almost gentle.

Coda, for Coda and Codette

Sometimes we could hear them through the wall,
the muffled noises of the twins, their names like
dragonfly fairies' names, Coda
and Codette—a boy named Coda. One night,
it was very loud, then very quiet,
their father was hunting them, with a knife,
they were hiding in the cold fireplace, behind
the fire screen. My mother never wanted me
to die. They were broken, in her, some of the
mechanisms of helping others
to thrive—she did not want me to thrive
more than she did, or as much as she did,
she had to triumph, but she wanted me
to breathe, even to sing, and my heart
to beat, without a quaver, except when she
appeared like a motorcycle Medea—
with something I would feel as intimately and
harmingly as she, in her turn,
had felt it—dangling from her hand. It was
her turn. But I think she never once
wanted to walk into a room and find me
cold and fixed in it. But I think,
for seconds at a time, when she was beating me,
I wanted my mother to stop being—
maybe to explode, I far enough
away that no speck of her could dart at me
and stick. I never knew when her eye
would fall on me, and narrow, and narrow, and
facets of sapphire fly out like friction
sparks. And our hearth was so small, no hiding
place except for a newborn—or before
a newborn, small as I'd been when I'd played
by myself in the dark heat, and waited
for her to draw me from inside her, and welcome me.

201 Upper Terrace Snapshot

When I see the sidewalk of San Francisco,
1945, under
the feet of the child, about four years old,
running, slowly,
toward the camera,
slo-mo loping, over the curved
surface of the earth, poured concrete,
scarified when damp—I turn it upside
down so I am looking down at my feet
moving in the soft, human-
scissors way, over the raked
whip-incised sidewalk. I recognize the sidewalk,
scratched in a wild, uniform taloning,
I know the high-top little leather
shoes, worn first by the firstborn, broken
in, made tender, then handed down
to the big-for-her-age feet of the second
girl, their soles scored, when new,
by the barbecue fork of the mother, so the child won't
slip-slide, I know the freshness and the
cruel-feeling care of the tines
which gouged the fragrant, tanned, animal
hide. I know the big-for-her-age
hand, dainty-cocked as she ran,
I know her sense of her shoulder blades,
her wish for wings. And she is like a large
faerie, with her acute senses,
bumbling flightless graceful over the
Roman hill of her oceanside birthplace,
her mother, with the two rows of breasts,
holding the camera. I know this child,
deer-shod, pattering up and down
the anticlines and synclines of the
port where the Pacific plate dives under as its
backside under Asia. I recognize
the fog in the air, the shining of her dark

hair that curls around a finger like a night wood
shaving, I know her thrill and fear
of being observed, the ecstasy,
to her, of being alive. And now
I cannot die without having seen her
loving her life, I cannot die
without having loved her.

Theme Psalm

There were corncob salt and pepper shakers,
and corncob napkin racks, and corncob
tea cozies, and picture frames—
the cabin where my father's parents
lived was chowdered with knickknacks in the shape
of ears of corn, because their name
was Cobb. Part of me, the Cobb part,
liked it, there was a theme to things, we were
linked to a real vegetable,
an archaic being like an ancestor,
a totem of golden nourishment, we were
kin to a pattern, a grid, a lovely
mounded and depressed order—
and part of me had seen my mother's
lip curl, when she saw the cornsome
bric-a-brac. The kernels of his genes
seemed to displease her—I think she saw them
in me, my DNA a maize
half hers, half wrong. But I loved to run
my thumb over the abacus glaze
of chromosomal grains—to know
I *was* my father, in a way my mother
was not, she was a Cobb in name
only. And it was a sight to see
my mother say my father's sister's
name, to see my mother hold herself
above such folly, she pronounced it like a sentence on
Cobbs: Cornelia.

On Truth Serum, Seventy Years
Ago, My Mother Chats

I can't say why I put it off.
Once I know she is waiting, many little
tasks crop up. And knowing she is there,
on the center of my rug, ready, gives a structure
to the house. I mount the staircase, south
then east then south then west, toward my door.
When I see her waiting, I sense her resistance
but I see she is naked from the waist down
and I know her resistance will break. I pull up
the chair from the sewing-machine console
and speak. I feel the hairbrush handle
in my grip, I feel the weight of the head
pulling it down from the horizontal.
She does not want to look at me—I say
Look at me, young lady,
and her eyes turn, until technically
she is looking at me. Then, at a signal
from the brush, she disposes herself across me.
Then there is a moment of completion. Then first
we get her attention—*koan*! Sunrise!
Cuts of the prism! Then we lead her into
the concept of duration.
I rain down, she is Saul on the road to
Damascus, I am the one delivering
more and more light on less and less
resistance, then, finally, she is singing.
Then she's my little girl again,
the house softens around us. And she's not
bad for days. I say, This hurts me
more than it hurts her, but in truth
it is good for both of us. If her father's
mother had only hit him, hard
and often! O give me more serum. I like
the turgor of that flesh, packed, split,

maybe with a little bowel movement in there,
and the spine, the spinal cord, and tiny eggs
like a world population. I like that there is
no hair, there are no breasts, it is
the essential totem human girl
and I am hitting it.

Run Away Up

What if I had run away up
from my mother—the last time she tried
to beat me—into the hall closet then
up the ladder and through the trapdoor into the
attic, like a spider running
up the sky? At least I did not
dive, headfirst, down the laundry chute,
into which my father used to
dangle me by the ankles, to fix
the fuse. I ran down the ammonite spiral
of the baluster staircase, through the dining room and kitchen, she
   caught
up with me
in the areaway
above the back stairs down into the basement with its
freezers and the furnace and the zinc sinks,
the room where "the Ironing Lady" did
the ironing. Maybe I'd been heading for
the back of the basement, to the door to the space
with floor and walls of dirt, where my father
had kept his amber bottles. Hana,
as my mother called her—Mrs. Oshida
to me—was the oldest person I had ever
seen, and she was not from here,
but born across the ocean, in Japan, and then
had come to California. I did not know yet
that she'd spent the war in an internment camp,
in a barracks, in the desert. But I could see
there was something about her which had nothing to do
with my mother, there was a whole world
which had nothing to do with the one who cornered me—
this first time that I had broken and run
as if I could not go through it again.
I think my mother could see that, could look
up and see it—she was now a head
shorter than me. And if I'd run up out the

top of the house, there would have been nowhere
to go but down onto the spiked fence—
or carried down, in a fireman's arms.
I had not thought of that! I can't
imagine shouting, Call the Fire Department
or I'll jump! As if a child could call on a
grown man to help her. I could have lain
down on the roof, while she called, and seen the
bright, connect-the-dots outlines
of the constellations, or maybe the moon—
the crescent, or the full—in which
Mrs. Oshida may have seen
a rabbit, and I a woman's face,
bent, in dignified mourning.

The Green Duck

In the dream, there was the green duck,
dark and small, wooden, worn,
made to fit in a child's hands.
In a way you could do almost anything to it.
But you would never burn it—the saints were burned
alive, they were very polite about it.
Maybe I was holding the cedar duck
when I first heard the word *duck*.
In the snapshots, I looked fresh, and my brain
looked as if it sparkled inside its shell.
Duck, it said to itself, and the duck
came in, like a welcome guest. I have eaten
brains, my tongue loves to probe
the delicate folds, and break my way in
to where there may have been dreams of calves—
some in the long envelope,
like a matter in a spirit,
some in the harness of the force-fed.
My brain is the home of a little thinker
with fork-lightning arms, and legs, and neck,
and hair. When I wake up, she is there
at the entry to her maze of beaten
paths. I try to guide her electric
boots over to the paths least beaten,
hills of the peaceable kingdom. *Duck*,
I say, she ducks, she gives me the Duck
of Death, and the decoy next to the clay
pool my father's father dug out and
liked to leave empty on a hot day.
There are homes where children are used as toothpicks,
sponges, razor strops, ballet
linoleum. I love you, I say to the duck,
and its green beak curves in a smile,
and it quorkles to me the secret of its young
night: You are going to have a wonderful life.

Dream of Mrs. Sly

Mrs. Sly, my first-grade teacher—
who told my mother, near my ear, I should be
spanked every day, as soon as I woke up,
before I had a chance to do anything—
would be sitting in my mother's driveway, on my mother's
Hitchcock chair, the one she tied me
to. The drive was overlooked
by Mrs. Baldwin's upper windows,
and Judge MacBain's—so Mrs. Sly
could be seen by the neighbors, wearing a billowy
nightie, a chiffon negligee,
and her breasts were outside it, horizontal, they were
undulating out,
in front of her,
on the air, as if resting on the swells and dips
of a creek—they were two feet long, whitish,
rippled like ribbon worms. And I was lying
across her lap, and she was rubbing salve
into my poor embarrassed enema-
hole. I hadn't heard of semen,
I didn't even know I had a girl opening,
but in that recurrent nightmare Mrs.
Sly was doing what she wanted with me.
Now I wonder if I'd liked something
about it—everything about it, my bottom
mooning the neighbors, the slippery goo,
the absence of pain. Mrs. Sly
was handsome, around 4' 11",
and wore spike heels to teach first grade.
I felt she hated me. My mother
did not hate me. She did unto me
nothing that had not been done
unto her, and she did not drive me crazy,
but just into certain corners of the human:
desire, exposure, shame, arousal—
and an unguent with millions of tiny people in it.

I Think My Mother

I think my mother had never met
anyone like me. Not her mother,
Victorian of corrosive suffering,
dead when my mother was seventeen.
Not her father, blue-eyed Quaker
in his Stutz Bearcat, dead when she
was five. Not her sister, or brother—
they all had those blue eyes,
as if they had fucked for hundreds of years
to develop that glaze, its pinnacle
the refractions of my mother's raking
lighthouse mirrors of diamond and sapphire
combined. "Shary does not have what one
would call conventional beauty," she wrote
in my Baby Book, "but when she smiles
her whole face lights up." I think she hadn't
met anyone who felt things
as intensely as she, and showed it. And she
had never been adored by someone so much
smaller than she, nor someone who tried so
hard to explicate to my mother my
mother's adorability, to
express in words and looks the ardent
preference the small heart
had for the big, troubled one.
Nor had she known
anyone who was
such a mixture of her and my father,
as if he had brought by force majeure
the rude glory of shapely buttocks
and long legs and curly hair
to bear on her family escutcheon. Nor was there
another person she had beaten. And there was
something not breakable in this girl,
something not quenchable in this odd,
funny, flirtatious child, her little

familiar whom my mother had pushed,
"right after a big B.M.,"
out of her body, as she wrote in my Baby Book.
She was so ashamed. Today I'd say
the birth-room smelled like a fertilized garden,
like pungent nourishment, and haste,
and eagerness, and hard work, and waste.

How the Buttermilk Was Administered to the Child at the True Blue Cafeteria

I don't think my father ever held my head back.
I do like having my head held back,
powerfully and not painfully, as if
hanks of my hair, and my lover's big fingers, have been
braided together, like spirit and matter—
I do not think
my father ever
held my head back, I'm grateful for that.
I think he simply told me, that if there is
a food you don't like, you will eat it till
you have finished it—so there it was,
at the True Blue, on the table, in the booth,
the glass of cruelly named *butter
milk*, two rights making a wrong,
and I had to swallow all the little
embryos, feel with the muscles of my
throat their tiny heads, spines,
teeny buttocks, and the soft claws that were the
tangles of arms and legs now never to have
life or will. He sat there, deep in him-
self as an unholy man
at the core of an unholy mountain,
down inside his drunkenness like a
fly in a log of petrified amber,
my father a representative of matter, like a
dream ambassador of death. Now,
I dip the tip of the spoon in the coffee if a
speckle of cream separates,
I pour it into the cone of grounds like
sanctified earth, I say *Go, and sleep
in peace*, and I bow my head, I offer
my nape, to the man I love, to be grasped,
he lifts me by the hair at the base of my head and
carries me out of this world, slowly,
through the extremest bliss of it
to a brief respite from it.

I Do Not Know If It Is True, but I Think

My mother beat me to the meter of "Onward,
Christian Soldiers." She speeded up
the tempo which dragged, in church—*Slow-ly
On-ward Bo-ring Chris-tian Sol-diers*—
and she got to give pain, maybe the same
pain her mother had given her,
and her mother's mother had given her mother,
and with the same Victorian tortoiseshell
hairbrush, one smash with every other syllable,
On-, Chris-, so-, as if
language as well as tenderness was being
savaged. She was back in the dyad, not
the bottom this time, but the top, feeling the
cuts at their originating end. I want
to gather the unaccented beats,
-ward, -tian, -o-ol, -ldiers,
and thank them, give them treats, whatever a
feminine ending eats, whatever a
half a pyrrhus delectates.
I cannot thank my poor mother
for beating 4/4 into me,
for fashioning me into her music box or to
ring her hour of grief for her,
making me her timepiece. "Here she
comes again, your kisser girl!,"
I'd cry out, as a small child,
to my mother—popping through a doorway toward her—
as now, toward you, out of my clock.
Lhude sing Goddamm. Cuccu! Cuccu!

How It Felt

Even if I still had the clothes I wore,
those first twelve years, even if I had
the clothes I'd take off before my mother
climbed the stairs toward me: the glassy
Orlon sweater; the cotton dress,
under its smocking my breasts-to-be
accordion-folded under the skin of my chest;
even if I had all the sashes,
even if I had all the cotton
underwear, like a secret friend,
I think I could not get back to how
it felt. I study the stability
of the spirit—was it almost I who came
back out of each punishment,
back to a self which had been waiting, for me,
in the cooled-off pile of my clothes? As for the
condition of being beaten, what
was it like: going into a barn, the animals
not in stalls, but biting, and shitting, and
parts of them on fire? And when my body came out
the other side, and I checked myself,
10 fingers, 10 toes,
and I checked whatever I had where we were supposed
to have a soul, I hardly dared
to know what I knew,
that though I had been taken down,
again, hammer and tongs, valley
and range, down to the ground of my being
and under that ground, it was possible
that in my essence, in some chamber my mother could not
enter—or did not enter—I had not been changed.

Easter Morning, 1955

Her appearance would be sudden—out from behind
the grandfather clock, a dryad squirted
from inside a tree-trunk. And she was so small,
the anorex had whittled her
to a twiggy nixie, she'd appear as if out of some
kindling dimension, her limbs not Easter
rabbitical but scrawn Blair Witch, she would
manifest, crying out,
"He is risen!" And we would respond, "Christ
is risen!" and she could intone, in turn,
"The Lord is risen indeed." I did not know
why she was getting narrower
and narrower, and drier, as I
began to odoriferate
and slop and bulge. I did not know
I hated—I did not know there was meanness
in me, and permanent dysforgiveness
and scorn. But, a month later, when her
brother asked for their father's clock,
and its innards were caesareaned out of it,
and its case was moved away from the wall
and pall-borne out of that home—when under-
neath where it had stood, heaps of years
of children's untaken vitamins
dully shone—on my mother's face was a
look of unalloyed regret,
and at that moment, from my narrow vision
of her, there emerged a slightly less
narrow vision—out of an
isosceles angle, an equilateral
angle was born,
as I had once
come forth from inside her with no thought of her, with
zero compassion—within me the means of the
invention of compassion and the means of its corruption.

Phobia of Red

Claret, burgundy, ruby, cherry;
hellebore, cardinal, heliotrope;
cerise, maroon, gridelin, carmine;
vermilion, magenta, scarlet, puce;
beet-, brick-, flame-, wine-:
it took me only fifty years
to know why I feared those colors. It was just
a single evening, when I looked to where
my father's face usually was,
to the left of his neck, after he'd gone
to the living room, and passed out on the couch,
and I saw red, saw a rumpled
sanguine mask, furrowed as if harrowed,
the inside showing on the outside,
the treasure taken from its bank and squandered.
I didn't yet know he had gone outside
and wandered, and fallen down some concrete stairs, I just
saw, for a moment, for the last time,
the beauty of our species' favorite color, and the
beauty shone about, silky and glossy, like the
light of the last sight of a loved
face before one dies—and then it went out.

Easter Morning, 1960

(Henry Averell Gerry, 1941–1960)

It seemed to me a mercy, that he died "without
a mark on him." I don't remember
who told me that, maybe one of his
roommates, who'd been in the car with him
and come through unscathed. A month later,
summer, they came to my home town, we drank
Paisano, and smoked Abdullahs
oval and pastel as Easter baskets.
And last night, I heard the word
windshield, and I suddenly wondered
how he could have been
thrown free
of the car, to lie, on the verge, dead,
without a mark on him.
And then for a moment I almost saw but I
would not see him, fontanelle
first, being born up out of the glass
into his fresh new death, his first
not breath, not heartbeat. And it seemed—
although it was not—like evil, for
his young head to be scribbled on,
defaced. But then I brought the shards
back together above the dash,
I drew in the web of the spider-line cracks,
and mended the car and him, and brought him,
whole, back down behind the wheel,
and when he swerved, and hit something,
his door opened, and he flew out,
asleep, his arms cradling his head,
and he fell to earth, and slept on the grass
for the rest of his life.

Cold Tahoe Today

When we go to the lake, I will see its colors,
moss green, lavender, sapphire,
the water I swam in at 8, 10, 12,
14. I would spend most of the day
underwater—then a forced rest
in the sun until my lips weren't indigo,
then under. I was an agate hunter,
a diver for transparent stone.
It meant so much to me to be
entirely inside that liquid world—
if my mother looked out from the rental, she would see
Tahoe. Today it will be too cold.
But I want to go in, and open my eyes,
and see the reaches of golden green,
and blackish purple—in solitude,
wearing the whole glacial cloak,
looking up, from inside, and seeing
the tray of mercury, the ceiling
to rise through,
the life to resume.
I do not know if I'm more afraid that I'll go
in, or that I won't go in.
I think it was like a sacred place.
No one could hit you, in there, no one could
pull their arm back fast enough
to strike. It was slow, there, there were
no humans there. And that last summer,
up on the land, they were still looking
for my classmate's body, she was buried, still.
I'd descend below the surface, and go
to the silence, to the unknown—life was
not what they said, and it was not what you thought it was.

Never Saw

I never saw my maidenhead,
I knew it by its resistance, it held
firm, a minor organ, a permanent
part of my body. The pain was so sharp
I felt disappointed, in myself, as if I was
not going
to be able to go
through with it. And his grunt of surprise—
his resonant, male grunt, so genuine, so
ordinary—he had not known
I had never done anything like that before. I was
months out of high school, it was still "going all the
way" for me, with this man from outside
the world I grew up in, who could have been sleeping
in the woods instead of in his car, as if he had
horns and a tail and hoofs as well as a
red beard and that bright-eyed laugh and those
paintbrushes and that zazen sitting-pillow.
And the blood, it was a flawless red,
so smooth, so bright, so much of it, as
if I was a natural creature, a
tree which swayed and almost spoke,
like a spring between rocks, up out of the earth.
Later, I would picture my hymen
as the soft bole or burl of a trunk, or as a
Boulogne oyster, with its papoose lump
on it, but as its wholeness was going,
and when it was gone, I did not miss it,
his getting rid of it was like cutting
my mother's throat without hurting her,
without her even knowing. And when
he did not call, when I did not see him
for a year, it was like the *Rose Fairy Book*,
he'd been summoned for a task and was completing it.
And nothing had been removed from me,
except the scarlet gush, and in it

a few cells of the torn edges—
I still had a maidenhead, split in half,
in a way I was still a virgin, but a virgin opened.

Sex with Love

When I look up Venus's eros-cone of a
skirt, like looking up my own skirt—
when I look up *Venus*, she is on the same
page as the cunning bivalve of
the flytrap, she is held in the fine
thousand layers, the *mille-feuille* of the
dictionary's petticoats—I find she was named
for *love*—for *desire*, its base "to strive for,"
"to attain." And suddenly I see I *do*
write poems in sentences—not broken into
lines, but wound around the caesura,
making a caduceus. And I see that desire,
for me, is bound up with the idea of the eternal.
I heard, in church, about ecstasy,
which seemed to lie outside dimension
and duration. And when I began to have sex-in-
love, it did not seem like something
I was doing—though it was—it seemed like something which was
happening to me, though I was striving
for it, within the gift of it.
And did I ever make love with anyone
I did not think I would be with all
my life? I don't think so. Sex was where forever
touched me, and I touched it—and where everywhere
burst, slowly, in me. It was the one
time in which we seemed safe from loss,
from parting, the hour when we seemed to step
outside time and space and everything—
outside our deaths, and the price of it was nowhere, and nothing.

My Father Happened on a Poem
of Mine in a Magazine

He wasn't supposed to know I was a poet,
but in his all-capitals block print,
he wrote me a note about something I'd written
which had lovemaking in it. When I was a child,
he would make night
fall before supper,
pulling himself
down from the vertical,
slowly putting the dizzy-ringed planet of his
head early to bed on the couch.
And in summer days, he'd reach up
under the outer cuff of my shorts,
and tug, once, at the hip seam
of my panties. Corrupted by his eros, I have sung it—
never, toward me, anything worse
than that. And when my puberty came, he showed
restraint, if not punctiliousness,
and not because of what I thought of as my ugliness,
it was more a matter of his carelessness and withdrawnness.
And now he'd written to me, "AFTER ALL,
I CHANGED YOUR DIAPER, I SHOULD HAVE KNOWN
YOU'D CHANGE TO KOTEX." KOTEX! In my
father's schoolboy printing! The X
of respects, and the boxing ring's KO,
and the menstrual text—my father said,
in Kotex code, I break the hex, I
brek-a-kex-kex, I bless your art,
I bless your sex.

Nemo me impune lacessit

When I learned of my mother's family's slogan,
I did not know that there were doctors who sat
on the floor, with a child, and a dollhouse, and played.
My outdoors dolls were a stick and a stone,
or a snapdragon and a dead bee—
one in each hand, they would shout at each other, in small
shouts deep in my throat. And sometimes
they shrieked, like the Medeas on the classical station.
There was nothing better, those hours with the under-my-
breath operas of anguish and death
and revenge, and the long solos when a piece of
dirt, or the corpse of a dragonfly
would pour out its story. And when I turned
to pencil and notebook, to lead and the pulp
of trees, I didn't yet know the motto—though she'd
had it punished into her, as she'd
punished it into me: *No one harms me*
with impunity.

The Enchantment

When I said, to my mother, *What was a good*
thing about me as a child?, my mother's
face seemed to unfurl from the center,
hibiscus in fast motion, the anthers
and flounces springing out with joy. *Oh you were*
enchanting, she breathed. *What do you mean—*
crazy? No sense of reality?
No-no, she laughed, with many little notes—
half a scale, plus grace notes—*I don't*
know how to say it, you were just . . .
enchanting. *Possessed?* I asked. *Brain-damaged?*
No, she smiled. *There was something about you—*
the way you looked at things. I thought I got it:
that stunned look on my face, in photos,
that dumbstruck look, gaze of someone
who doesn't understand anything.
But a week later, I thought it had been
a look of wonder, bemused pleasure.
And days later, I see it—that light
on my mother's face—she loved me. And today
I hear her, she did not say *enchanted*.
The woman in whose thrall I was
was in my thrall. I came into being
within her silks and masses, and after we are
gone would she caper here, my first
love, would she do me the honor of continued ensorceling?

Like a Sonnet

My mother might be in the room with me, but she was
like something in the next room, and like
something downstairs, and something down the street.
She was like the bridge the next-door mother
jumped off, and like the sea, the horizon,
and Cassiopeia. My mother was like
the chair in her room with a shellacked seat,
a chair which was like a saddled horse.
Simile was a way to get
away, you were safe as long as you did not
go too far, over the edge
of sanity, into metaphor.
My mother was *like* a mother; she was
not a mother—no, my idea of a
mother was like a mother, and my mother was a mother.

Varicosonnet

When I was a child,   I thought the fine,
vertical, snaking,   blue-green line
on the inside of my   mother's right leg
was a sign of womanly   beauty. And I felt,
the way my luck   went, that I might not
get one. It was   like her own
Nile, privately   owned—owned
by God, worn   by my mother. I did not
hear anyone   talk about
my mom's goddess   likeness, chartreuse
Loch Ness rippling   up toward her between-her-
legs. But when   I had carried my kids
to term, I learned   my mother's varicose
vein was a sign   of maternal service. Thank you for your service.

From the Window of My Home-Town Hotel

On the lee slope of the small coastal mountain
which conceals the sun the first hour after its rising,
in the dry, steep ravines, the live
mist of the heat is seething like dust
left over from an earlier world.
A crow with a swimmer's shoulders works
the air. And a little bird flies up into a
tree and closes its wings, like a blossom
folded up into a bud again.
In the distance is a very old pine, now sparse
and frail as if hand-painted on a plate
washed for a hundred years. And the bell
in the tower, which rings the hours—the rhythm
of its intervals is known to me.
I am forgetting my mother. It well may be
some fur of her marrow is in a steep
trough of fog aslant in a gouge
of these hills—her bones were pestled in this city,
down the street from this hotel,
after her face had been rendered back
to her God. I don't sense her here.
At moments I picture my young self,
that long, narrow chin pointed like
a mosquito proboscis. She knew this place.
This is where she saw the grindings of the
femurs and ulnas breathing in the air,
and the crow's work by which it earned
its eggs, and where a songbird seemed
a flower again, and saw a tree
worn away by human eating,
and the double notes of several metals'
struck resonance waiting in what had
been them, before they were belled from the earth.
She wanted what was not there, and she saw and heard it.

My Poem Without Me in It

My poem without me in it—would it be like
my room when I had returned to it
after my mother was done with me.
Under my bed, only the outer
space balls
of dust, only
the asteroids of hair, no bent-legs-
spider drawstring purse, no fly, no
I. My poem without me in it—would it
be like her house before I was granted
the right to close my door—it had been one
hive, one queen five times my size, her
long stomach lolling like a tucker-bag.
My poem without me—like the mahogany
bookcase, with its spiral pillars,
without a book by a woman in it.
My poem without
a simile in it.
My poem like my head, as a child, when I learned
how not to have
a thought in it,
in case it were a thought one would burn for.
My poem without this ordinary female
in it—like the body politic
of a teenage woman without her special
blood in it. This old girl's
poem without a girl in it.
I have been a child without a soul.
The poem is a vale of soul-making.

Where I Die

In the mystery, when people are emptying
the dead one's home of all traces of him,
I suddenly see that this small apartment,
this pair of rented rooms, may be
where I die. I picture a couple of strangers
carrying me out, I'm on a stretcher, in braids—
somehow I'm a skeleton already,
smiling, and probably wanting to get up
and cakewalk out, as if I could still
amuse someone, with my song and dance—
an articulated puppet, who could make it
look as if I'm having fun, as if
this is what I had had in mind,
all along, before I was born,
when I was a soul raptor, hovering in the
vestibule above existence, and I
saw, far below me, the edge
of the Pacific, and the Golden Gate,
and my parents' roof, their ceiling, their bed,
their bodies—and saw inside their bodies,
inside her, and inside him
inside her—and then I was tilting and peregrine-
stooping, and diving into being! I want to
have as much fun on my way out
as on my way in,
as if this whole thing were my
idea, a little comedy
between nothing and nothing—between everything
and everything.

The New Knowing

What Thou Lovest Well

And then, in the night, I wake up, and I can't
remember how I met my ex,
and I think: I let a stranger into
my life. Then I remember we met at a party,
he was the friend of a friend of a friend—all
medical students, which seemed, to me,
those days, as if they were bonded and insured.
But I did not know him. Suddenly I under-
stand that my parents were strangers to me—
like a pair off the street, I took them in,
in a wave of alchemy, to the cells
of my body and brain, I gave them fresh being,
I did not know who they were, and when they
showed me who they were, I did not believe it,
I would not know them, I kept them strangers,
I would not see them—and my chosen mate,
I could not, or would not, know him, and
we cannot love what we do not know, or we
cannot love it well enough. "What thou
lovest *well* remains, the rest is dross
What thou lov'st *well* shall not be reft from thee
What thou lov'st *well* is thy true heritage."

Remembering the First Time

It was after the birth of a child, it was in that
small, dark, back room,
deep in the building as a kingfisher's summer
tunnel in the bank of a pond leading in
to its nest of eggs, it was in that slight
feeling of sadness after coming, and then it
came up from inside the earth of my body,
it wasn't sadness, it was more desire—
and that desire, from within the satisfied
desire, broke
with the force of both
desires—and then, after brief rest, rose
higher, deeper, and broke harder, longer,
and then another, and it went on
awhile like that, until the changes
had been wrung from the whole cloth of a life
up to that hour. And of course I thought it
was love, and it was. And when we unswooned,
the world was not the world I had known,
and I wanted to go and stand inside
a blossoming fruit
tree, a cherry,
and look up,
into it,
and see the bright ganglia
of blue sky, and the many gathered
skirts of the multiple blooms—I came to,
there, where I would spend my life,
decades more with him, then decades without him.

After Divorce

Once a year, in the park, for an hour,
we'd meet, and to see his face again—
the skin like a ceremonial sand garden,
known grains and new grains
raked—known and new lines
of thin and coarse tines, the rubble of
time stopped down—was to feel like a desert
dweller, in the desert, at night, looking up,
seeing the tiny pocks of impact,
the gravel and shrivel of the surface of the moon,
and feeling at exile home. We would chat.
I would waver on easier—*It's easier,*
this time, to see you. But it was—the space
between us got a little firmer and firmer,
its air thicker, a barrier between us
like a mesh of spore in a petri dish; and as we
walked to where we would part, it was between us
like a low wall, which moved with us,
accompanying us. He said, sounding
surprised, that I looked good, and I said that the
part of me that does not know
where he went, is always relieved
to see him, there he is! Alive! And then,
we'd get to where we would part, and there'd be a
hug, like a child embracing a tree, and then
one went one way, one another,
one in sheer relief, one
in grieving relief.

Where Is It Now

The heart of my life was spent on it—
that was my life! And where is it, now—
as this train goes down the mountain for an hour,
six years
after divorce—
all that sex, it must be somewhere.
Maybe among these wild grasses near the
tracks, or near plants in the sea which drink
salt like milk, as if the scenes of
impermanent love could be stored in tide pools'
gardens, where a mountain steps down into the
sea, then down into the ocean trench, until it
touches the spherical mountain which is
the mantle of the globe. Or maybe where seeds
fly without catching, until they turn
to fray—maybe where the children who die before
birth live, or the creatures who die before
conception. Maybe the love made, within a
love that was not lasting, moves in
huge discs of dust beyond our
solar system, but I think not,
I think those kisses, and little gasps, those
sighs and long samurai strokes,
and breast-tips leapt to hardness like sudden
horns on the brow of a milk-fed goat—
I feel it is all nearby, in the hair of the
woods this train now passes, and it lines
roadsides, I can hear the insects singing
in the nerves of the meadow, the made love of a
life is the inner logic of a life,
the home fragrance.

The New Knowing

What we had done, my ex and I,
for decades in our bed, didn't feel like something
we did, but something passing into us,
through us—taking the shape of space
and time. And it seemed to be all one motion,
from before the beginning to after the end
of it, we stepped into the stream of it—
we eased in, between the double jump ropes,
and helix-jumped, for unseeing joy,
and in service of what joy is in service of,
the brute continuance. I can't
remember what it was like, after
he left, the coarse fur of the floor
against my cheek. And when, a year
later, I fell in love, in crush,
in paradise squeeze—I felt dumbstruck with amateur
luck. And yet, when I heard the new voice,
in the bed, I knew. When I heard the caressive
words, I knew—the generic names of
affection used, the bee's word,
the sugar's word, I knew his terms
of fondness were impersonal,
a traveler's names for whatever town
he is passing through—once again,
I had stepped into a stream, this time
alone, into the river of a man's life,
the waters where I'm called out of my name.
I heard it the first night, I knew
what I heard, I turned my green back
on my knowing, I labored with him for days,
weeks, months, a year, we made
not war, not love, but temporary
powerful sweet sorrow.

First Boyfriend After

I had liked him as a friend, and as his child's father,
I liked that he asked me out the moment
he heard that "that guy" had left me,
then I liked that he liked seeing us,
that time the closet door was open so the
mirror on it faced us, I was on
top, we were about to come,
and he said, in joy, "Look at us, Sharon,
we are *fucking each other!*"
Maybe his most conjugal moment,
that whole year—sometimes at parties
he seemed to me to be pretending we were not
there together. And sometimes, in the bed,
eyes closed or not, he seemed to be
looking more at himself than at us, or as
if someone else might be looking at him,
as if he was performing for them.
There was joy between us, even a kind of
innocence, and there was irony,
and the opening of the iron privacy
about our parents. "They tell you once,
and if you do it again, they kill you." I was not
his observer, I don't know who I was,
or what, was I like the air
he moved through, like the water the sea otter
streamed through, the oxygen from its fur
seething—was he playing me, was I
his instrument, the air thru
the flute, or the flute with its fierce shrieks
and stops, did he play me, sweet music, as I
am playing him here?

Boyfriend Blues at 55

It's as if, with him, I was always hiding,
somehow—even while lying behind him,
in the bed, in those long stretches of the night,
laid out, full-length, parallel behind
the opulent tumuli of his body,
I was always slightly afraid. Mostly,
I thought of dangers to him, as he did,
as a free being is dogged by the fondness
of others. So I'd lie pretty still, and attend
the concert of his snoring, as if I were hearing
the edges of the solid world
torn by the liquid. All along, I think, somewhere
deep inside him, there was a pool
where the flame of love was brought, and carried
low to the surface, so it shone doubled,
it beat like a creature flying, and then
it was lowered in. And my task was
to pretend the doused fire could rise
out, again, as if the soaking
surface were a flint—
my task was to witness the refusal of love
and to assist at it.

Boyfriend Lament

And when it is a month since I have seen him,
sometimes I miss my ex-boyfriend's curves
themselves—haunch, buttock, juicy
chest, shoulder—as if I am
a geometry shrine, which the curve visits.
And then I give in, and think of his blunt
feet like feet encased in feet—
fleshy insteps I had pressed with smooches
in the early days, when he seemed to like
being loved. And then the warrior legs,
their intense shapes—and then child lid your
eyes before the hex's arcs and pinions,
tangent and hypotenuse
of the text of Elysian theorems, now sealed.
And the belly—beggar desire—and the thick
small of the back, and the spinal brain
where the parents are held, and the parents' parents
rule. And at the breast, turn
your eyes away, it is an auricle,
vestibular soul candied forth.
If it was to be all matter, no spirit,
some can do it, but I had to leave it—
break the sweat of my longing on the scatter of
moles on his throat like summer hayballs
on a distant slope, break the balls of my
heart on the little hill of vine-knots
in the armpit, where love's grapes, where dust,
where musk, where palate-burst—go up to the
pillar of the throat, to the nape,
the ear holding close to the head. And now,
I see his closed mouth, and his eyes
open at the surface, but somewhere in the iris or
pupil, where I used to bend upside down and cry
out, shut. And for a moment I see him
as he was, closed, I see him as if without
reference to myself, almost without mourning.

Maybe a woman's grief for herself,
one woman
after another,
is the shrine he visits.

Go

"Go, litel bok, go, litel myn tragedye"

Geoffrey Chaucer,
Troilus and Criseyde

Then a hard-boiled egg from the fridge, peeled,
revealed, on its slope, a body hair
from my post-marriage ex-boyfriend, the coiled
o of the last few loops of its tip. It looked
stalwart, and energetic, it looked
magic from the birth-lips of the chicken. Half
a year since his touch or sight—half a year since I
swept the kitchen—where now, in a web,
suspended like a relic in its glory, is the cursive
scrawl of another nether hackle.
Have I learned nothing, that I want to make
a shrine for it,
as if one keratin effluence,
blah blah blah, of his matter, is an icon
and my spirit is its worshipper?
As if I am not worthy so much as to
gather up a crumb. I'm standing near the toilet
holding the intimate ringlet when I suddenly
see it: hoarding, and grief, and rage,
and longing for the unloving,
lie close in me.
Joy to the fishes in the deep blue sea.
Go, little hair, go, little my tragedy.

When My Fear That I Won't

When my fear that I won't
slough off the fat
that I slabbed on, with my heavy boyfriend,
evaporates, I recall my body
from 16 to 64,
limbs shaped and lean as kitchen
utensil handles—spatula;
slotted scoop with six entries;
long-tailed spoon to sup with the devil—
and when I moved around, the lengthy
oak and cherry wands would make their
music like the drawer with the eggbeaters and the whisks in it.
To think, with the extra off, I am going to be
delicate again, sklendr in an elder's
way, angled, planed—a thrill
trills through me,
remembering those almost fifty
years of love's making, without an
ounce of fat between muscle and bone,
having the pounce factor of a panther,
an *once*,
carrying the treasures of the breasts, the magi
punchbowls of the ass, the trove of the mound in
front, down there, which, in my dreams,
as a child, was pale green, and translucent, and luminous.

Unexpected Flourishing

For a crone bald
at both ends—
her neath-her pate
as well as her above-her—
to sing the merkin would be one thing.
I sang it when the bird could still be
heard, in the bush, trilling in the curlicues—
and then the deforestation of the moist
mosses, ferns, and soft lichens .
progressed. And I'd appreciated—
sixty years ago, when I'd
begun to sprout a little woods—how
bushy-tailed I was, the sweet
cloud of the bunny's dark puff,
on me, in front. Years later,
when I was approaching the last exits
of middle age, when time was smoothing and
denuding me—
though my body and soul
had their eye
on a man—there suddenly rose up
delicate coils of black bedsprings
from out of Venus's mound on me,
the fresh spirals of a woman in her late
prime. Whether we ever or whether
we never, I gaze down at them now
in wonder, the darling tiny bellpulls, the ringlets of bright dodder.

Elegies

1

Hospice-Bed Song

I did not hear it, leaning over
the hospice bed, when my sister and I
had our mother among our many
arms and hands, that brigantine, that little
caravel out on the water for its last
journey, back to her dead departed
before her. We were bending over the small
vessel of her, over her crow's nest,
from which, toward the finish, she seemed to begin
to see the blue border of reunion.
She did not sing it, but she had sung it,
I will arise and go now,
all my life she had sung it—all *our*
lives, my sister was also beside her,
but whenever I was with my mother,
there seemed to be no one there but she.
And a small, cabin, build, there—like her
God, when he squatted, like a woman, with the clay
and wattles, and started to make people.
Now we were at the other end, there was a
wind in that room, rising, falling,
our girl was shoaled, she was waiting for a tide
to float her keel up from the rock and coral.
And we did not hold her back, though we held her so she
would not be without company as she
made her way to her native shore, where she had
come from. Her face became smoother and smoother, *for
peace comes dropping slow,
dropping from the veils of the morning,
to where the cricket sings*, she lifted
free, in the salt air on our faces,
silent, silent, in the quiet room,
no breath—she was there, at last, in the pure
matter of the world, *in the deep heart's core.*

After Closing Up My Mother's House

Last thing, at dusk, I leaned out
the hotel window, like a seal sticking halfway
out of the concave comber it is riding.
To the west, the slopes of land offshore,
violet mist, like isles of the blest
seen by a child of genteel flogging,
and the water looked horizontal, a shining
scale balanced. First thing
in the morning, I leaned to the waist out into the
cold dawn, and rotated east
toward the rim of coastal mountain toothed
with sequoia and pine. And a crow cried out
in heavy vigor as he beat along
the face of the hotel, and when he came to me
he shied, going up on his hind legs
like a rearing stallion. All was in place—
the fitted box of the planet, the tiered
sewing-table town. And when the van rushed me down toward the
tideflats, the sun came over
the ridge to the east, its traditional direction,
as the parent, most of the time, dies
before the child. We passed the room
where she had breathed her last breath into
my mouth, I could not save it, I do not
know where it is—
not in space, but held, by the weight of our
natal stone, within our homemade
atmosphere. And we passed the cottage
with the cobalt window,
and I muttered what her children had shouted here, *Blue
Window! Blue Window!* Along the runway,
wind poured through the coat of horsetail
fur, and terns, in their skirts, fluttered
above the thumbnail and crochet-hook snails,
and we knock-swashed up, excreting fumes
of carbon fern and marrow—and in

the seat pocket, in front of me, were
crimped, furled buds, stems
bushy with fresh thorns,
and her last flagon of perfume, its glass
dove alighting to seize it, or lifting it up.

The Relics

1. Brett Returns My Mother to the Wilderness

I slipped them into my friend's palm—
the tiny crucifix, and dove,
from off my mother's pendant watch—
and I asked her to walk them up, through the brush
toward timberline, and find a place
to hurl them, for safekeeping. Now
she writes, "I walked up the canyon at dusk,
warm, with a touch of fall blowing down the canyon,
came to an outcrop, above a steep
drop—far below, a seasonal
creek, green willows. I stood on a boulder
and held out my hand. I wished your mother all the
love in the world, and I sent the talismans
flying off the cliff. They were so small,
and the wind was blowing, so I never saw or
heard them land." My mother is where
I cannot find her, she is gone beyond
recall, she lies in her sterling shapes
light as the most weightless bone in the body, her
stirrup bone, which was ground up
and sown into the sea. I do not know
what a soul is, I think of it
as the smallest, the core, civil right. And she is
wild now with it, she touches and is
touched by no one knows—down, or
droppings of a common nighthawk,
root of bird's-foot fern, antenna of
Hairstreak or Echo Azure, or stepped on by the
huge translucent Jerusalem cricket. There was
something deeply right about
the physical elements—atoms, and cells,
and marrow—of my mother's body,
when I was young, and now her delicate
insignias receive the direct

touch of the sun, and scatter it,
unseen, all over her home.

2. Cross and Dove

I had not wanted them, and I hadn't known
what to do with them, the minuscule
symbols of my mother's religion,
I looked for a crack in the stone floor of the
cathedral but could not find one. Then I thought
of the wilderness near Desolation,
and asked my friend to carry them up
to a peak of granite, and let the wind take them. Since
then, it has been as if my mother's
spirit matter has been returned
into the great bank of matter,
as her marrow had been sifted down into
the ocean. It doesn't matter, now, if I
ever wanted to disassemble
my mother. The sixteenth-of-an-inch-
across cross, and the silver line-drawing
of a dove are cached, somewhere, that is nowhere
to be found. Now I think of the nature of metal, and how
long the soul-dolls of her trust will last in their
spider-egg-sac of roots, needles,
quartz, feathers, dust, snow, shed
claw. Her belief she would have an eternal
life was absolute, I think.
It would not be good to think of my mother
without her God—like a hermit howling in the
moonscape of a desert. Once, when she was old—like an
exquisite child playing a crone
in the school play—we talked about heaven.
She wasn't sure exactly how, but she
knew her father would be there, and her elder
brother, and her second husband—

maybe it was a heaven for four,
the three men and her. It was so
easy to make my mother happy
in her last years, to tell her that I
could just see her, as a kitten, in God's
lap, being petted. Her eyes sparkled with more
beams than any other eyes I have seen.
I have sent the tokens of her everlasting being
into the high altitude.
They will shine long after I can sing her—sing what I
perceived through the distorted prisms of my vision.
I don't know if I saw my mother
or did not see her. Day and night,
her charms will gleam in the brush or stream, will
reflect the mountain light in little
pieces of unreadable language.

Dawn Song

An hour before light, in the overcast,
in the high curds, is a slight glowing.
I can hardly say what it was like, to look
for my mother—to be watchful for her face in the house,
and then, in her face, to look for her altered
face. The glow, over the horizon,
flows, as if the moon is riding
on something. I'm seeking the hard, bright
arc of her jaw, which year after year seemed
smaller, as my own jaw grew, so that she
became, over time, like a child of whom
I went in fear. And now, behind
the curdle, a rim rises, toward a clearing,
and the curved sphere appears, and slides,
and slithies—a crescent, its points down,
its insides fallen down out of it.
Boil the water, pour it on the tea,
begin each day with fresh milk.
I bring it to the window, to the western gate,
and the little singing visage lies,
whitened by morning, on the back of its skull,
singing and sinking, spare with a skeleton's self-
sufficiency, with the truth of harmless
peace in death. And I want to say, to my
mother, my journeying laborer
who wandered here, with me in her hobo
sack—I want to put her to sleep
like an exhausted animal. Sleep, baby,
Sleep. Our cottage vale is deep.
The fearsome lamb is on the green,
With woolly fleece so soft and clean.
Sleep, baby, sleep.

Her Birthday as Ashes in Seawater

By now, my mother has been pulled to the top
of many small waves, carried in the curve that curls
over, onto itself, and unknots,
again, into the liquid plain,
as her ions had first been gathered from appearances
and concepts. And her dividend,
her irreducible, like violet
down, thrown to the seals, starfish,
wolf spiders on the edge-of-Pacific
floor, I like to follow her
from matter into matter, my little quester,
as if she went to sea in a pea-green
boat. Every separate bit,
every crystal shard, seems to
be here—her nature unknowable, dense,
dispersed, her atomization a miracle,
the earth without her a miracle
as if I had arrived on my own
with nothing to owe, nothing to grieve,
nothing to fear, it would happen with me
as it would, not one molecule
lost or sent to the School Principal
or held in a dried-orange-pomander strongbox
stuck with the iron-matron maces
of the cloves. My mother is a native of this place,
she is made of the rosy plates of the shell
of one who in the silt of a trench plays
music on its own arm, draws
chords, and then the single note—
rosin, jade, blood, catgut,
siren-gut, hair, hair,
hair—I miss her, I lack my mother, such
peace there is on earth now every
tooth of her head is safe, ground down
to filaments of rock-crab fractals
and claw facets, the whole color wheel

burst and released. Oh Mom. Come sit
with me at this stone table at the bottom
of the Bay, here is a barnacle of
egg custard, here is your tiny
spoon with your initials, sup with me
at dawn on your first day—we are all
the dead, I am not apart from you,
for long, except for breath, except for
everything.

In the Temple Basement

Standing in the ladies' room line,
in the temple basement, the woman in front of me
said, "I've been sitting behind you, admiring
your hair." "Thank you! White for Rosh
Hashanah!" I say, and then, "It was
a gift from my mother." I love to say
my mother to someone I imagine as a normal
person—though who knows. And I love
to see cut flowers age—we are cut
flowers, when they sever the cord, we begin
our dying. She lived to be 85,
I needed every hour of it.
Each time I made her laugh on the phone,
that warm gurgle—and she couldn't reach out with her
long curved polished nails, to stroke me—
we were making something together, like a
girlmade mountain stream among
Sierra onion, and lupine, stonecrop
and Leopard lily. And especially
I needed every minute that last evening,
watching her, watching over
her—and beyond her harm!—and wishing her
any good thing, including more life, though she
began to look serene, her lungs
filling, rattling, ceasing, starting, but her
spirit was on its way, and since she had
always believed it, and I think could not have
borne to live without it, it was as
if she was nearing the blue home
of her heavenly father, and then finally opening into
permanent blossom.

Let the Night

Four in the morning. Let the night
creatures walk—snow-footed ferret;
bobcat; shrew; mountain lion;
lynx; paw, claw, skin—
and let my mother walk, with them,
let her, come back, in, again,
for an hour. An hour is a long time.
Let her come back in for fifteen
minutes. A lot can happen in fifteen
minutes. Let my mother come back
for a silent run-through of Onward Christian
Soldiers, like the song in the back of her mind
she seemed to have been beating her daughter to.
And she enters, out the side of the coastal
mountain onto the bare porch, she is
five or so
inches tall,
and comes in with a hand resting, on either
side, on the shoulder of a long-haired rat. O
approach, feral queen, my thick glass
door is locked, I can see you through it,
greenish, pretty as a shepherdess,
a rat-herdess—don't mind
that rushing above you, it's just the great-horned
owl. And now there's some shimmer before first
light, some shed petals of the day
to come. So if you've had enough,
for now, of lording it over creation,
may I suggest you go back where you came from—
back through the mattery door of lordation
and longing. For the dawn is at hand, the dawn is at
arm's length. When my mom was in
a stroke trance, years before
she died, and did not know me, her mien was
cold, indifferent—profile
of the lingcod's sister the electric eel.

But when she was on her death bed,
her face, in coma, glowed, its skin
shone with joy—it was the elements,
receiving themselves back again from her
borrowing, earth's darling,
fire's young, air's child—the
little legions went from her then, on their
quiet nocturnal feet, breath after
breath, foxtail plume from her soprano
mouth, opossum breath, ringtail
mouth, pocket gopher breath,
until her whole creaturehood
had been returned to its originals, and I
saw her there, mortal as they come.

As If My Mother

When I realize my mother is one of the women
in history who has had the most poems
written to her, it irks me—as if she was
conducting music, or science, when she was
beating on me. What was wrong
with my family, the generations of mothers
beating the daughters—and what was wrong
with the men. My mother nursing—
her breast as representative
of the female, the doe, the mammary goddess—
has been sung. And her singing, her sharps and her flats
have been sung. When I was born, there weren't
a lot of songs of women doing
what my mother had done—given birth,
nursed, bled, beaten one
of her children, as her mother had beaten one—
always the second daughter, the second
one who had been supposed to be
a son. When the farmer beats his wife who
beats the dog who beats the cat who
beats the mouse, who does the mouse
beat? She does not beat her young.
Maybe she beats the catskin drum.
Four! beats! to a line! and I'm done!
I'm putting it here as morning comes,
as the full day moon is going down
into the mountain, deposited,
dissolving in the light, mouth open, eyes
open unseeing. When our species began,
language and tools and ritual burial
began. I want to bury my mother,
if possible, with both truth and honor.

Blossom Trees

They seem to be gliding toward me, in dresses,
they float and turn, in summer floral, the
ladies of the fruit trees, in ruffles, in dishevel,
they are like the prettiest mother in the class.
And every bouquet on their batiste is like a
nipple, a puckered ruby, asking
for the pierce-kiss. My mother seemed
to long to be dandled, she seemed terminally hungry.
Held close against her body, I was
pressed into human anguish, its blooms
and prickles and raking thorns and hazy
generalized wounders, pressed into the service
of her grieving orchards. Now, when I see
a blossom tree, I want to match
my apple or witch-hazel arms to it,
I want to be the blossom tree
as I wanted to be my mother, throw my little
spirit into her, to ease
the sorrow of her matter. And there were her breasts,
always, two storms of petals, each with its
chipped, faceted, girt cluster
of rasp and black and boysen nectar,
I do not think I ever forgot them, I
think there was no break in my memory.
I pass by their ghosts, now, their soft-shatter
revenants. Are we here to prepare
for our death, to begin to make our farewells as we
arrive—do we exist to mourn the earth?

Holding to a Sea-Wall, Treading Salt Water,

in my dream, I turned my back to the ocean,
the Pacific, which behind me went to the horizon
and beyond it, following the curve of the earth
down, the water holding to
the earth. I was going to swim back to land, but I
felt the sliding body of liquid
around me big as my mother when I was
an egg inside her, a blastocoele,
a tiny seahorse embryo.
What if my mother
could have been happy
if I hadn't been born, what if she could have
become an opera star—and never
gone flat!—would I abort myself
if that would have made her success possible?
People would die for their kids, my mother
was the baby I grew in, and emerged from, and took
care of as if I were a punishment child whore—
couldn't I give up my life for her?—and for a
moment I did, at last I had
the power to make my mother happy.
I cavorted, quietly, in the swell,
with the embryos who had also chosen
their mothers' lives over their own, we were as
safe now in matter as we would have been after
our death from old age. I floated like a lei in the
wake of the boat from which we had let go
her ashes, and most of the blossoms from her garden.
At last I had not ruined her life, I had
set my darling loose, to sing like a god.

Where Is My Lady?

I don't know where the moon is,
four in the morning. Orion is out,
faint. For how many years was he my bright
imaginary husband—much colder and more
distant than the imaginary husband
I was married to. And in the years by myself,
inside this house in sight of no other
houses, in the dark, hours before dawn,
I would look up, and out, from behind
a window, at the black tray
fierce with gems, and I'd feel I had to go
out and stand under it, though afraid
there might be a human male on the loose
in the woods around me. Now I think
maybe the heavens' intense glitter
was like my mother's eyes when she was so much
taller than I, and she labored to put me
out in the wind, unprotected,
as she had been. Well, I attend
the moon—and not as a monster, I await it
almost as an equal, a companion in space, once
part of the earth until knocked away.
This very early morning, I do not
feel I do not deserve to live,
nor need I scare myself by going
out where our unnatural species
roams. But where is my lady? Is her autumn
parhelion so low that she's behind the hill
to the south? My mother is losing great
chunks of her power over me,
a decade after her death. I had not
run a visionary hatpin through that scarcely
fleshed creature into the hospice
mattress, nor would I have detained her, she was so
ready to cease to tarry. I never
tied my mother up, I never

had her in any pillory
till now, I was always at her beck and call.
Now, it is as if I have
my mother on a delicate dog-lead,
Belt of Orion—whenever I like, I
tug, gently, and bring her reeling in.

Where She Is Now

When I think of where my mother is now, I don't
think of her in the air, though she is there;
nor do I think of her in fire,
though a cinder speck of her stubborn delicate
jaw may remain in the iron trough; nor in
earth, I think of her inside
the sea, in pieces—each piece
my mother, now, or what passes for her
among the ions and animalcules,
atoms of spiral narwhale horn,
crystals of salt, dollhouse cubes
of sugar held out to a seahorse muzzle,
velvet lips among the diatoms,
broken diadems of bone—
when I think of my mother, I see her doing
little jobs of value, tiny
polishings, her return into matter
honorable. Probably it means
I wanted, at certain times, to explode her,
to dash her to pieces—as in *The Messiah*—
like a water vessel. Now I see her parts
dreaming, dusting, down inside
the open ocean, a grain of her burnt and
pestled occipital bone in a tiny
apron that has pictures of squid on it and
housewife octopi, eight-tasked—and
now I feel I'm telling a story to my
mom, to make her laugh, to let her
know that I know that she did, against
the odds, her best.

Double Elegy

When I was with my parents, at their deaths,
in the last hour, both times,
my spirit was holding its breath. We were out there where I
did not know where we were, as if our
matter were space, near the borders of its passage into
nothing—there were planets, workaday,
rolling silent by, and luminous
moons, their backs to us, and troughs where
atoms turned inside out. I was there to
guard them as they were changed, my spirit
was in their service, but my eyes—my eyes
were holding them up like the hams and canned
yams at the altar at Thanksgiving, to be blessed;
my eyes were loving the feared houses
of their heads and faces, the hide tents,
yurts, translucent igloos of a child's
nomadic life,
but also my eyes were watching them die.
They had been there, laboring in the dark, when I came to
be, and there when my scalp, with her blood
on it, first peeked, and then came in,
and now I was there at their going out,
in the classic order, the parent before
the offspring. And when they had died, my eyes,
like feral shine from beyond the fringes
of a clearing, were seeing them dead, seeing one
turn to a white and the other to a green
orchid, and later, one to a yellow
lake and the other to a golden, dried
sea, and at last to a cloud in the shape of a
skull, and to a cloud in the shape
of a pelvic cradle,
I saw them turn to things I had cherished
in their places, things in which I had stored
their imagined love of me.

My Parents' Ashes (New York City, October, 2001)

Maybe they have touched, by now.
Maybe a grain of my mother's bone,
cast in the Pacific a month ago,
has glanced along a grain of my father's,
loose in the Bay for twenty years.
Maybe a molecule of her
has lain beside a molecule
of him, or interpenetrated
it, an element of her matter
bonding to an element of his,
sodium on potassium,
calcium on magnesium,
Ossa on Pelion, maybe they
have even shared an atom together,
Na, Ca, Mg, or Fe, with its
2 electrons in the K-shell,
8 in the L-shell, 14 in the M,
2 in the N, as if they could circle one
nucleus, like parents a crib,
share an atomic weight, their cold
embers conjoining alkali metals
with earth metals on the periodic
tidal table, as the currents carry them
back and forth under the Golden Gate.
Ashes are *the solid residue left*
when matter is burned at not too high
a temperature. A molecule
is *the smallest particle into which*
a substance can be divided and still have
the properties of the original substance,
my mother's dust, my father's dust,
ghost legs of the spider crab
picking its way along the rock sea floor. *If the*
substance were divided further, only atoms
would remain. They died, old, in my arms,
the gift of their last breath went into

my mouth. They chose for their bodies to be burned
at the heat to preserve their grit, they chose
the ocean, chose not the weather of the day
but the words said as the gray fur
blew from our hands into the cradle of salt—
an easy death, and in its way
an easy life, no one they love
vaporized, the dream covenants kept.

2

On the Bank of the Columbia River

Often, yesterday, I was not
sure she was breathing. Her hand was warm
and hard in my hand—her fist resting
in my palm, my thumb a little roof above it, I would
watch for the tiny amphibial leap
in her throat. The bridge which spans the river
is not her age, 102, but
the sluice-walls, and the cement piers,
show the stains and layers of their ancient
sedimentary pour, maybe a
hammer dropped
into the jellied
concrete, maybe a shoe.
                        Suddenly
I want my baby shoe, to give to my
late father's almost late
wife, a craft to pole across
the river in. On the far side,
the shack above the water rests on shale
slabs, or old, silvery boards,
and above the horizon a V of geese
swags, dips, double-Dutches,
drops a line down through a line, not a
whip's lashes, no driving hand,
no will enforced at one end,
received at another—this is my step-, my
non-violent mother—the hieroglyph
darkens above the drink of water of her
fierce elongate body.
                        If I wanted
to seek something to thank for the days
alone with her in her last room,
able to answer any question,
able to sing the old songs—
Tho the days are lonely, sad the nights and long,
I would need to look no further than this west-flowing

water, or the mountain it descends from, or the glacier
which carved the mountain, or the volcano
which had lifted it up, or the hot spots on the plates
which had glided here, out of the ridge
in the center of the ocean, or what lay beneath
the pouring-up split in the ridge, or what lies below that.

Morphine Elegy

(for F.L.D.C.)

And now our girlish one, our lady,
one hundred and two, is being given to the one
to whom we seem to give everyone.
She and I, three decades ago, were in
the room with her husband, my father, for his last,
quiet hours, his animal eyes
open without sight—each shot into his
IV tube one more push away
from shore, to put him to sleep. And my elder
sister, and I, had said the word
we hated, we'd prescribed death for our mother two
decades ago, when we understood
that death, and the morphine which would bring it on sooner, were
all that stood between that frail
powerful creature and pain. And now,
for another mother in another bed
it is called on, again, and slowly
her memories are being folded
and put away, they will never be taken
out again, and shaken out,
and gaze-caressed, save by their god,
Morpheus, Croesus of the last
hives of honey and venom. First the outer then the
innermost corridors of the brain
are stilled, and cool, resting on the not
sweet, not bitter, the neutral shelves of the
irrevocable—no way for any of it
to happen once more, no way for it not
to have happened. She is curled there, living treasure, we
live within her still, we rise and
fall with her every breath. We will stop them, when we
see, of pain, she's had more than enough,
and then we will live on her breaths for the rest of our lives.

Last Day with My Father's Wife

(for Frances)

When I stroked her head, down into her neck,
she held quite still, as if feral, and I realized
I had not touched her much, except for
hugging her, and kissing her,
and maybe she hadn't been touched much
in the 102 years of her life,
except in her first marriage, or when
my father had been with her. He'd appeared to her
with the same dark, brown, eyes,
and the same first name as her young husband
who had gone the way of their firstborn who had not
breathed the air of the earth. Today,
our lady had cast almost everything off—
even her upper teeth, like a wing picked
clean of gristle—white incisors,
canines, primaries, secondaries,
intact, a pinion removed from her mouth.
I hadn't known that she still had small brown
boulders set into her lower jawbone, like
stones in a field worked by a tenant farmer,
as if her life had not belonged to her,
but was something chosen for her by others,
a labor performed, not without joy,
unpaid, and now she is laying down
equipment and skills. Most of the day
I held her hand, which was holding its thumb,
and I sang to her, and when I sang,
a look of wonder would come over her head
and face, as if who had ever heard
of such a thing,
and then, as the day wore on, she would sleep, and I'd
read, and my head would sink, and suddenly I'd
jerk awake to the sight of the long-limbed
golden wrecked dragonfly

on the hospice bed. And I'd sing, again,
Desert sil'vry moon beneath the pale moonlight,
Coyote yappin' lazy on the hi-i-i-ill,
the phrase rising like a swimmer through water,
her body brought closer and closer to a shore
where its elements will separate
and return to their sources, and the notes will come up through the
air to cluster in the concave curve
of the atmosphere, like grapes beyond harvest,
the others having been dropped, by her,
one by one, into my father's mouth.

3

Burial Day

(for Galway Kinnell)

He is still above the earth—I mean
aboveground, above the horizon of the earth's curved
rim. He spent the night—his body
spent the night in the barn, upstairs,
in his study, the coldest place indoors—
wrapped in a blanket. And Fergus and Gwyn
dug the grave, the shovels biting down,
topsoil, sand, granite, and Maud
washed his body, and with Tune Maud made
the box. They will place him in it—may be
lifting him now, gaunt moonrise over
the ridge, he lying inside the growth rings of
pine, they may have set the lid and he
may, this moment, be sinking down
through recent geologic layers—or some
ancient ones thrust up, there may be a
piece of a nautilus shell, from an African
ocean, being firmed over him.
O rest. The table is not far,
where the discs of the bases of the wine glasses made
hypotenuses with the variable surface
of the rock. And I wonder if the world is not silent—
to be inside of—if it groans, if it creaks
as it turns. I know there is no one there in him
to hear it if it does, I know the slack
or rigid, lax or flexible, husk
is not he. Nor is he the one
lying between the pages of the books—
but open them, he will rise up
and sing. And he's the one down inside
the vinyl trench, whom the needle will quicken and we'll
hear him again. I am daydreaming, it's so
quiet, here, hundreds of miles
from where they are setting the mortal part of our
Green Man into the Green Mountain.

Big Boy Blue

Big boy blue, when you were born
did you weigh ten pounds, or a dozen? And were you
the color of a summer sky
till your big lungs took your first
February first breath? The fire,
this morning, looks like hair, growing
fast motion and writhing. When you were a child,
did you look at a mother with writhing snakes growing
out of her head? You did not turn
to stone, but to language, you turned to air
and water with the wind's writing on them.
When we first met, you seemed like a wolf in wolf's
clothing of beauty, a man with the fresh
ancient mouth of an early singer,
a man who was ready for a woman friend.
Above the pond, this morning, there are figures, bent
forward, made of breath, going east
from west, as if on a long march.
Wherever people were walking for freedom,
you would walk with them. Old Man Blue,
the sheep's in the meadow, the cow's in the corn,
the beaver is moving slowly across
the upside-down sky, through the clouds, trailing
her cape of wake. How can it be
you are not in the world, only your long
husk, your music all poured out,
safely decanted, into the rich cold
cellar of reds we would drink and describe—
a cabernet with the bouquet of a
school playground in the rain, after
the bell has rung, a sauvignon like a .
No. 2 pencil lead, stabbed decades
ago, into my knee, or the salt
and money Odysseus smelled on the side of the
sheep. I'm blowing my horn for you,
again, in a world where you cannot hear it—

you are supine, washed, clothed in linen, being
lowered into the mountain, like an underground
stream, we will come put our ears to your chest
the rest of our lives. The sheaves are in,
the sun is setting, like a meteor, deep
into the earth, and where is the one
we love? the one who looked after us?
He is under the haystack, fast asleep.

Landing in San Francisco on the Way to the Community of Writers (with a line from Tom Waits)

When I emerged through the oval hole in the side of the fuselage,
there was the old smell of home: sweet
diesel, and the faintly rotten Bay.
When you reach into a cardboard box of human ashes,
you drive soft shards of ground bone up under your fingernails.
We dropped fistfuls of my mother through the rising and falling
      surfaces of the swells.
Across the continent, the towers were intact,
as if the footage of a few months later had been run backwards,
ashes to flesh, ashes to floors and ceilings.
Thousands of families in the dream of the ordinary,
of having a body which would remain whole during death.

First light the next morning, a figure of smoke
is walking out a long pier over San Francisco Bay,
followed by a dog of smoke.
No, it is a coat of ashes
and a cat of ashes—
Hash browns, hash browns—
it is a man pulling a cart out to the fenced oval at the end of the dock.
He unpacks, and starts praying, and another man comes, they are
      singing,
no, they are fishing. Galway, I'm glad
you were buried whole—as little of you as was left,
it was all of you there was,
deep in the ground on the slope of the mountain hillside,
and you called all those who could come, to come to you,
the carrion and death-watch beetles, and the worms you loved to
      honor,
the insects and bacteria and molds and spores, and,
close enough up, they could be heard at their work,
chhhrrrrrrrr, gsmck gsmck gsmck, j-j-j-j-j-j-j-j-j-j-j,
so your body could sing its way into the earth,
so your fellow creatures could dance you back into matter.

Song to Gabriel Hirsch

We first met in your home. Outside,
summer fire. Inside, Texas
summer ice, I was wiped out
by travel and illness, lying on a couch,
which made me a good height for you to talk to.
That I had a son, with the same name
as you, struck you with wonder—me, too—
one name, one label, two beings. We said,
to each other, I think, whatever came into
our minds—put there by what the other
had just said—as if we dropped,
one by one, taking turns, those
intensely dried paper flowers
of my childhood, into a glass of water,
and watched them uncurl, fast, uneven,
and bright—and tossed another. We were in
the present moment, so intensely in it
everything outside it took a step back,
out of the light, then another step back.
And that was where we met, next,
years later, in that light, you were so
intent, alert, alive, as if
in the grip of a fierce brightness, and moving
around in it, quick in its grip. I wish I had
been there, last week, to hear your best friend,
who had met you eye to eye—in what,
in your childhood, was the future—talk of how
extraordinary you were, my almost
unknown dear, your mother's and father's
dearest. You were wearing a cape, that first day,
a cloak of many colors, a cloud,
your hand on the shoulder of the wild creature of your life.

Tory Dent Elegy, Big Sur

Every year, the dead, head-down-the-
cliff pine nurses at the base of the
cedar, drinking from its feet—cedar
that bursts in a bark firework from the cliff—
and along the arms of the sheer-drop dweller, on its
wasted biceps, the eight-legged fishers cast
their nets, cauled with fog prisms and with
six-legged foods. Every year,
the surf, below, milks the edge where the
Farallon plate of the ocean floor dove
under the Nacimiento plate
of the continent, plunged like a freight
express train down, several inches
a year, and still plummets, the ocean's
wet rear upending here like the
backside of murre, otter, seal,
cormorant, gray whale diving. There is musicless
song, down there, atonal, coming
up from salt beating on stone,
beat without melody, mineral percussion,
as matter, like a sadist, played on your darling
bones, wherein you lived, and can play no more, as if
someone pulled, at the last moment,
an instrument out of a fire, dear heart,
our Strad, its strings your own guts
drawn and dried before your eyes,
its bow-hair your fallen-out glory, God damn it,
you sang, in your chains, for every thief
crucified, for every King and
X hash-hashinated, for every
Shepard hung by butcher birds from the
wire, for every whole note
hung by its rope from the score, for every
child who drank gas at the manicured hand of the
gasmonger—O Victorine,
you held on, in love, to sing,

gnashing lies till they were dead, shaking the
lies' bodies to be sure they did not
twitch, ferocious huntress. When I was a
child they would ask us sinners what the
fuck we would say when brought before God
on the last day—and now I know, by the
green chainmail needle, by the thread
of sexual fire, by the gray lion's spots; by the
boulder's head and the foam's silk, I would
say I that I knew you, and then I would sit Him
down and feed Him, forever, Black Milk.

Garlic Elegy

Dear Ruth, while your best beloveds were returning,
to the earth, the stunning vehicle
which you rode through time and space, I went
to the window, with a bouquet of garlic
from Vermont—the kind called Music. The stalks
were dry and leggy, noisy as husks,
and the heads hard, and out of each
top, a wild tangle of fine
shimmying worms. Down in the park,
a mockingbird flashed, gold-gray on his breast,
her breast—two breasts! Your body, your bones
and terrestrial organs, were going home, into
the ground of Goshen, and your words were staying
up here with us. You had your dashing
mockery, but you didn't copy
anyone. Here, sweetheart, run
a fingernail along the dent
between two cloves, let the papery tissue
rustle and leap aside, and here
we are, the teardrop nugget in its loose
amber hide. Then I fixed it for us
later, I fixed a whole scepter-
ful for us—pungent sixths,
rogue open intervals, which had come
up out of the globe, which your long,
musical tag end was being
lowered into, past the bazook
roots of the sod, down past
the glacial rubble. We'll join you, there,
as we joined you here, opening our beaks, and you would
drop a morsel in, which we
would turn to fledgling flight, along
the long, impermanent—the mortal—
songlines of the air.

Sonnet for Joe of Nazareth

Suddenly, it strikes me that Joseph
was Jesus's biological father,
denied by his son (who thought he was adopted)
and by Mary, who believed she had slept with God.
How can it have taken me
5/6 of my life (if I get to be 90)
to feel for Joseph, wounded in
his sense of fatherhood by his son's
conviction that he himself was divine.
I want to thank Joseph for the hard
work of his hammer, for every dwelling
he built, including the body of his boy
who was sure he himself had invented matter
and spirit, and eternal fire.

Morning Song

Do you remember the layout of the rooms here, dear one?
Rooms lit with 8,000-foot light
reflected off granite. To each of us here
you were a different dear one—
but not a shapechanger, you were yourself,
Pawtucket periodic table of elements.
Do you remember the first time we met?
You wanted to meet me to see if you wanted
to teach with me. You sat in your chair
at your desk, in your office,
I sat on the low couch, and looked down, and
saw I had forgotten to shave my legs,
there were little hairs like commas scattered all over them.
Those days, I sat up straight as a seraphim.
I don't know who I thought I was—
I think I thought I was your guardian angel.
And the language we spoke together,
it would have looked like the pages we faxed back and
forth nearly every day for twenty years,
our duet, rewriting each other's poems—
marks of our old portables' fonts, with serifs,
and marks hand-gnarled—ammonitic, pure black with fax-ink,
vined and doddered among the ribbon-banged lines.
I had never met anyone who longed so desperately to make
            something—
a call, a set of cries, a world.
Sometimes I felt sorry for you about your beauty,
it got in the way of your truth—it was part of your truth,
but it got in the way of your human ordinary-enough-ness,
as if you were a hybrid species,
something feral in the set of your head and eyes,
and in the animal connectedness and quickness of your hands and
            feet.
That was your problem, or your joy—my job
was to see your poems were not too beautiful
to be true. And after the years of your centaur driving—

you part of the car, part of the road and the lowest sky—
those years of pressurized cabins, and university auditoriums,
now I do not know where you are.
O I know your body is under the hill,
near the surface of it, six feet below
the grasses your feet pressed on the way to the stone table with your
        love
—your body or whatever is left of it,
your long bones, the rest streaming as if
singing out into the Vermont topsoil,
and I know where your words are, with us,
but it took me so long to unlearn hell and heaven
that in the broader story I cannot find you,
except in the hummingbird standing still on the air facing the aspen
        leaves—it avails,
and the yellow-orange tank truck reversing up to the lodge doors—
        it avails,
and the soft cry behind it, "M'om back, m'om back."

Stanley's Mouth

(for Stanley Kunitz, 1906–2006)

Then during the long afternoons,
I end up spending a lot of time
looking into Stanley's mouth,
waiting for the next word,
contented to wait. I like looking at his
teeth, like landmarks of a loved terrain,
native quartz, or oak, or pier, "When you
wrote 'The Portrait,' did it seem like a new kind of
poem for you?" I ask. *My father*
killed himself, Stanley says,
before I was—then the small ocean
and shores of his lips and tongue, and their surrounding
silver whisker, work, B
for Boy, B for Bobcat, I watch
the plosive begin to come in, sea hem, and
pull back, and come in, and then wash all the way
in, *before I was born,* he says,
and in public. From the beginning I felt I was—and we
stop, again, on the blunt sill
of that consonant, he falls back, and then
comes forward again, *born into sorrow.*
"Not depressed," I say, and he says,
In so many ways I enjoyed my childhood.
"You knew you had come to the right planet,"
I say, "you were at home here." *The first*
thing I did when I wrote it was read it
to my mother, he says, *she didn't say anything—*
she wasn't a responsive person—
but I saw her tension as she listened, and then
she took it into her room with her.
"Giving her child his freedom?" I ask. *I felt*
punished, Stanley says. "Not guilty,"
I say. *I never even MET*
the fellow! Stanley exclaims, and I say, "You mean

punished sort of as in original
sin," and he nods, behind him the green
haunt of cypress, cedar, lavender,
alyssum. And his mouth, mouth of a working
poet, works, again, on that early
building block, in pulses like the rhymes
of the tide—he once again moves toward
the beginning of the first word,
the closing of the musical old
lips, without sound, again, again, then,
Born into sorrow.

Animal Crackers

I liked to bite the hindquarters off the hippopotamuses,
and the humps off the camels. I loved tails,
and ears, like those of the hollow chocolate
rabbit who appeared in my house when Jesus rose.
The indented spots on the leopard sent me,
the deep engravings in the zebra's side . . .
Sometimes I liked to save the head, then
pop it in and attend, to feel
that brain of dumb sugar and flour
added to mine. And now that I am half
old, I want some poet crackers,
some Smarts, some Whitmans, little busts or
cameos of everyone,
to eat. I ate Christ, and the bunny,
I want a Levine matzoh, I want
Dickinson by her own recipe,
and Keats, bright oatmeal brooch. I need to
read, lip-read, tooth-read, Ruth
Stone, Miss Gwendolyn Brooks, oh sweet
salty Rukeyser cracker! And I would like
to be one, to be in those little boxes
with woven handles like shed snakeskins—
edible Kinnells, Cliftons, and Kunitzes!
I wish, when I am dead, I could be
among the English and American animal crackers.

Song Before Dawn

In the dark, not the full dark,
woken by the cold, pulling the covers
up around my mouth, making a small
cavern of warmth, of living breath,
sensing the over-under of my sleep-loosened
braids—all my arms and legs
tangled around each other—I used to
lie on this mountain, and Galway and Lucille
were dreaming nearby. I used to put on
layers and layers, by touch, and despite
my fear of being outdoors in the night—
as if I were not a person but an occasion for violence—
I would go outside, the sky black,
as if, if there had been a God,
it might have petted me on the head,
like Galway in his scrupulous mercy toward me,
like my chivalry toward him,
and our confiding in each other like a child in the woods
confiding, without language, in the needles and cones.
In the dusk before first light, above
the granite domes which look from here like
peaks but are the knees and hipbone crests
and clavicles, jaws, occipital arches
under the mountains' fontanelles,
the stars are still just visible,
and in the binoculars clear and sharp—
but despite my holding the heavy lenses
leaned against the stucco frame,
my tremor shows each star swiftly
whirling in a white-gold ring, like Saturn's,
in one direction, then swerving, then the other,
then an hourglass, a spiral, a bedspring—the stars
sparkler-tracing my shaking. And now,
in the quietest moment, the voice it took
the earth millions of years to speak,
the vireo before first light.

When my hands were steady, I would stand at Lucille's
shoulder at the lake, and softly pluck insects—
nine-spotted lady beetle,
giant crane fly, green darner,
black snow mosquito—off her
shoulder, nape, whitecap, and blow them
out over the glacier-blue water
toward the place where we're going, one by one,
two by two, sometimes many
at a time, someday all together, as if reunited.

Vigil

Sitting on the floor under the window, near midnight,
in the Valley, 6,000 feet—around it
the peaks of 8,000 and 10,000, looking up,
aslant, waiting for the late moonrise—
the mountain and the dark sky
looked like a slope of solid rock.
Every moment, I thought she might appear, our
deep step as if high in the air now come
shining. The boughs of the pine—under which we had
sat, beside the columbine—
the spaces between their needles now looked like the
shirr of mare's tail. I gazed where I thought
she could arrive, my face close to the cold pane,
and a bat like a heavy butterfly,
with small, surprisingly ample breasts,
rushed at me and swerved so I cried out and pulled back and came
forward, my cheek against the chill glass,
then smaller wings fluttered and affixed,
and opened the graceful shape of a death's-head
moth. And then, two thousand feet up there,
just beyond the crest, between the Ponderosa
trunks, there was something like a brilliant sugar
or salt city, wet conifer bark
in full-moon glaze, I held my breath
in case it was the first
silver drop
of the arc at the top of the sphere, which it was not.
It did not rise. I was craving to see
the rim—and then to haul the whole
orb up! After a while,
I sat on a chair, my feet on the sill, far
under the gleaming ridge of the vertical
horizon, and waited, and did not mean
to sleep. Then I woke. The field of black
bathed with milk—nothing, no one,
as if she was never coming back. And deep in the

valley, in the shadow, I laid down a path of my
clothes to the bed, and went down, into sleep—the last
known location of her soul, the place
she left from—I went to that place, and lay down,
at its sill, at its shut door, for what remained of the night.

Sacred

1.

I heard the word, a lot, as a child, I
do not know what the word means.
I think it has to do with awe,
or terror. Sometimes, walking alone
in the dry, coastal Berkeley Hills, I'd
enter a grove of eucalyptus,
ivory yellow-green peeling gray skin,
and stop, as if something was with me, or I
was with something—if the earth had a spirit,
non-human, not-god, made of itself. And in the
minutes after my father had died,
his body beginning to return to its elements—
becoming not a being, but a former
being, like a thing, a huge, cut flower,
even though his heart was still beating,
minutes after he had stopped breathing,
and after my mother had started to slightly
glow, turning into an ecstatic, without
air, it was like those clearings, as if something
was there though her spirit was no longer confined
there. She was free of her life. But to awaken
in the prime of your life, beside your beloved,
the great, wry, passionate soul who
adored you above all others but your shared
child, and to turn, next to you,
in the bed, and see her in her full beauty,
and to reach and touch her, and to feel that her body
was cold, and still,

that is a place
only one
goes, one now holy living
being, who holds her whole life,
now, in his, as long as he both

shall live—that space is now sacred, the shape
of air made between them, the shapes
they make as he takes hold of her;
the music of extremest shock
and grief is sacred, I know that I may not
go there, I cannot, this is a song
of not going there,
to the house, the room, the bed, which eros and now
pure loss and solitude have made
consecrated, inviolable.

2.

It would not be possible for anyone
but him to approach that moment. I don't know
much about love, about decency. If I'd
been anywhere near—what do we
do, when there is nothing to be done—
I could have stood,
outside the door,
like the child John Keats, Junkets, age 6,
standing outside his dying mother's
bedroom door, his wooden sword
unsheathed. Maybe other people
know what it is O.K. to imagine—
decent people. And yet the aloneness of the
sufferer is so terrible
we wish we could keep them some company
in it, even though we know we cannot.
To wake, next to one's life, one's co-
creator, and look at them and see their perfectness,
home at last. The end of the world.
I don't understand character,
or dignity, or the individual,
or the soul, or decency. I want to
accompany my friend's suffering,

to drink some part of it for him though it
cannot be done, dive into salt
and swim through salt to them and give the
cross-chest carry, and scissors kick and
bring them up into the air. Tonight
I can see wanting to spend one's life
in silence, to honor the unspeakable.
The living lover who has woken beside
the body of the beloved is holy. Everyone
knows to keep silent in their presence. But at
the grief service, the woman with red
here and there on her black-and-white
kimono moved, she brought touch
and touchlessness, presence and absence,
heat and cold out of her body
into the air
so we could breathe it,
wishing it were she
who could breathe it,
so many there that night would have changed
places with her, for her to walk in, again.

First Child

The First New Human Animal

The first new human animal
I saw in my life was you, and you had
the neonatal smallness and roundness I'd been
formed, in my own unborn brain,
to cherish. I could see, in the first days,
that you'd been—not folded, but compressed into a
shape to be carried in a limited space,
your ankles curved in like closed wings, like the
slithery crowding of those sweet-as-heaven
peach halves, in the cans of wartime, with the
picture of an orchard on the label. I feared
I might be as unlike a good mother
as the picture of a cling fruit
in corn syrup was unlike the pit
and skin on the tree. I did not go around
thinking about my mother,
but I lived and breathed her. And now I was
what I'd feared. And your shocks and shudders at the external
world—the cold, the hunger—it was
as if I was hearing a child crying
in the wilderness. We were alone together
all day, week after week. When he'd
get home after work, around 7, or 8,
it was easier, two against one,
and during the night he'd get up and go get you
and bring you in, and fit you to me,
the two parts of the puzzle in his care.
It got easier—but this was my life now,
my life. And then—you don't remember
that day, but it's within you—you looked at me,
and looked away, and looked back at me
and smiled. And my whole life wheeled
around and began to move in a new
direction. It was you! I had not known
who you were, until then—I had not known it was you.

When You Were First Visible

When you were first visible to me,
you were upside down, not sound asleep but
before sleep, blue-gray,
tethered to the other world
which followed you out from inside me. Then you
opened your silent mouth, and the first
sound, a crackling of oxygen snapping
threads of mucus, broke the quiet,
and with that gasp you pulled your first
earth
air
in, to your lungs which had been
waiting entirely compressed, the lining
touching itself all over, all inner—now each
lung became a working hollow, blown
partway full, then wholly full, the
birth day of your delicate bellows.
And then—first, your face, small tragic
mask, then your slender body, flushed
a just-before-sunrise rose, and your folded,
crowded, apricot arms and legs
sprang out,
in slow blossom.
And they washed you—her, you, her—
leaving the spring cheese vernix, and they wrapped her in a
clean, not new, blanket, a child of
New York City,
and the next morning, the milk came in,
it drove the fire yarn of its food through
passageways which had passed nothing
before, now lax, slack, gushing
when she sucked, or mewled. In a month's time,
she was plump with butterfat, her wrists
invisible down somewhere inside
the richness of her flesh. My life as I had known it
had ended, my life was hers, now,

and I did not yet know her. And that was my new
life, to learn her, as much as I could,
each day, and slowly I have come to know her,
and thus myself, and all of us, and I will
not be done with my learning when I return to where she came
        from.

First Child

For three years, two months,
two weeks, no days,
four hours, five minutes—
mostly with just the two of us there—
in the presence of our daughter's beautiful
brain, soul, heart, face,
body, I became a mother,
a tender of the brand-new,
a learner at the soles of the feet,
on the old white-painted changing table
of the very young, the one whose mind
received hundreds of fresh cells
every day, like what at playschool they called
"mine *from home*." Our girl was the first
human I got to get to know a little,
before she was born—and I learned her without
knowing her gender, she was the first
purely human creature whom I
experienced—and inside me, so I learned
her motion, power, need, four-limbed-
ness, and her head, which I pushed like my own skull
down and out through the pain of the earth,
the maliceless pain of being. And there
she was, no one I'd imagined, but the one
who was, for part of a second, the youngest
person, perdaughter, in the world. We lived
from persecond to persecond, I in fear
and awe, both of us in shock
and startle, she in a blur, her recent
developments—hands, fingers,
thumbs—in the dark, now becoming
visible to her. Without words,
she knew to miss the heavy, soft
liquid of her first home, and she
was not the core of my being, though she was the
purpose of my being—she was her own

core, and I was still my own soul. It was as
if I had never understood anything,
before, and now I understood
a little. I stood in ignorant bliss
and terror and held her up, changed her,
deftly slowly put her jamas
on, gave her a nightcap of milk as she fell
back near her
original light-
lessness, and I poured her into her crib, and in the
hours of my sleep listened for her,
for those years, months, weeks, hours,
forgot her only briefly in the new baby's making.

Aria Conceived in Mexico

Our first child was my first contact
with the other world—which had been, all along,
this world,
inside myself.
Our child used to not exist,
ever, and then, over sand, under coastal
trees, near breakers, she came into being, came
out of the world of nothing, the world
before time, before death,
into the world of time and death
and love, in a country of poetry
and courage, of guarded riches and unguarded
poverty, on a beach in the Republic
of Mexico, she entered this
dimension there. We did not know
who she was—but, slowly, I learned
motherhood—it was her life now,
not mine. I'd been an envelope,
and now was a living basket, for the civil
holy, the new life. And the milk
arrived, hard, in what had been
my breasts, and now were for her, and the other
world sent out, through them, food
of this world for her. And she slept, and the smallest
motion of eyelash or hand was the meaning
of my life. I would kneel at the bars of the old
cradle and listen for spider sight
and warbler pant, and lobos moan.
And the other world had sent in, with her,
her means of continuance, the tiny
fresh eggs in her first-breath side.
Through her children, her life would continue,
and maybe, if we do not destroy
the earth, it too might continue, the whole
life of the human, in Bahia Sur,
and Mérida, and Islas del Mujeres.

Acknowledgments

Grateful acknowledgment is made to the editors of the publications
where some of the poems in this book previously appeared.

AGNI: "Burial Day," "Gliss Aria," Hyacinth Aria," "Like a Sonnet"

The American Poetry Review: "After Divorce," "Anal Aria," "Big Boy
Blue," "Easter Morning, 1960," "The Enchantment," "Garlic Elegy,"
"Graduation Aria," "How the Buttermilk Was Administered to
the Child at the True Blue Cafeteria," "Let the Night," "Mourning
Undone," "The New Knowing," "On Truth Serum, 60 Years Ago,
My Mother Speaks," "Stanley's Mouth," "State Evidence," "To Etan
Patz," "Unexpected Flourishing," "When My Fear That I Won't"

The Atlantic Monthly: "8 Moons"

Black Renaissance Noire: "Cervix Aria," "Easter Morning, 1955," "Sweet
Land of Liberty," "Where I Die," "White Woman in White Makeup"

Brick: "Aria Above Seattle"

Calaloo: "Song Before Dawn"

Five Points: "Dawn Song," "My Parents' Ashes (N.Y.C., October,
2001)," "Timothy Aria"

Gulf Coast: "Cold Tahoe Today," "Departure Gate Aria," "Morning
Song"

Harper's Bazaar: "Apocalypse Approaching as I'm Aging"

Harvard Review: "Where She Is Now"

Lenoir-Rhyme Magazine: "What Thou Lovest Well"

The Los Angeles Review of Books: "Early Pastoral Aria," "Pasadena
Aria," "Theme Psalm"

Narrative: "After Closing Up My Mother's House," "Holding to a
Sea-Wall, Treading Salt Water," "Kunitzeiform Aria," "Nevada City,
Calif., Aria," "Scrapbook Aria"

The Nation: "Silver Spoon Aria"

The New Yorker: "For You," "The Green Duck," "Her Birthday as Ashes in Sea-Water," "No Makeup," "Q Aria"

The North (U.K.): "Sepia Aria"

The Paris Review: "Birds in Alcoves," "In the Temple Basement"

Ploughshares: "Meeting a Stranger"

Poetry: "How It Felt," "Poem Which Talks Back to Itself," "The Relics"

Poetry London: "Phobia of Red"

Poetry Review (U.K.): "Bad Boyfriend Lament (or Go)," "Bonnard Aria," "I Do Not Know It Is True, but I Think," "Scansion Aria"

Prairie Schooner: "As If My Mother," "Dream of Mrs. Sly," "Never Saw"

Sewanee Review: "Aria to Our Miscarried One, Age 50, Now," "A Pair of Sonnets Against the Corporal Chastisement of Children," "Remembering the First Time," "Vermont Aria," "Where Is My Lady?"

Southampton Review: "*Breaking Bad* Aria," "Morning Aria, 6,000 Feet," "My Father Happened on a Poem of Mine in a Magazine," "Rasputin Aria," "Sex with Love"

The Southern Review: "First Breath," "Song to Gabriel Hirsch," "The Task of Naming Me"

The Threepenny Review: "Bay Area Aria," "From the Window of My Home-Town Hotel," "Last Day with My Father's Wife"

Tin House: "Animal Crackers," "I Think My Mother," "Landing in San Francisco on the Way to the Community of Writers," "Looking South at Lower Manhattan, Where the Towers Had Been"

"Immigration Aria" appeared in *Resistance, Rebellion, Life: 50 Poems Now* (Knopf, 2017).

Sharon Olds was born in San Francisco and educated at Stanford University and Columbia University. The winner of both the Pulitzer Prize and England's T. S. Eliot Prize for her 2012 collection, *Stag's Leap*, she is the author of eleven previous books of poetry and the winner of many other awards and honors, including the inaugural San Francisco Poetry Center Award for her first book, *Satan Says* (1980), and the National Book Critics Circle Award for her second, *The Dead and the Living*, which was also the Lamont Poetry Selection for 1983. *The Father* was short-listed for the T. S. Eliot Prize, and *The Unswept Room* was a finalist for the National Book Award and the National Book Critics Circle Award. Olds teaches in the Graduate Creative Writing Program at New York University and helped to found the NYU outreach programs, among them the writing workshop for residents of Goldwater Hospital on Roosevelt Island, and for the veterans of the Iraq and Afghanistan wars. She lives in New York City.

A NOTE ON THE TYPE

The text of this book was set in a typeface called Bell. The original punches for this face were cut in 1788 by the engraver Richard Austin for the typefoundry of John Bell (1745–1831), the most outstanding typographer of his day. They are the earliest English "modern" type design, and show the influence of French copperplate engraving and the work of the Fournier and Didot families. However, the Bell face has a distinct identity of its own, and might also be classified as a delicate and refined rendering of Scotch Roman.

Composed by North Market Street Graphics,
Lancaster, Pennsylvania

Printed and bound by Berryville Graphics,
Berryville, Virginia

Designed by Michael Collica